MW01093976

Ordained Women
in the Church
of the Nazarene

Ordained Women in the Church of the Nazarene

REBECCA LAIRD

Nazarene Publishing House
Kansas City, Mo.

Copyright 1993
by Rebecca Laird

ISBN: 083-411-4526

Printed in the United States of America

Cover Design: Crandall Vail

Unless otherwise indicated, all Scripture quotations are from the King James Version of the Bible.

Permission to quote from the following copyrighted version is acknowledged with appreciation:

The *Revised Standard Version of the Bible* (RSV), copyrighted 1946, 1952, © 1971, 1973. Used by permission.

10 9 8 7 6 5 4 3 2 1

For Rachel, my daughter, whom I carried
while I came to know and love these early
women ministers. May your life be blessed
with the strength, boldness, and wisdom
that characterized the lives of these foremothers of faith.

CONTENTS

Acknowledgments   9

Introduction: Some of Our Best Men
    Are Women   11

1. The Changing Role of Women
    in the 19th Century   23
    The Changing Society of the 19th Century   23
    The Separate Sphere Doctrine   24
    The Women's Movement of the 19th Century   25
    The American Holiness Movement   27
    Theological Beliefs of the Holiness Movement   28
    Antoinette Brown Blackwell and Women's Ordination   31
    Phoebe Palmer and Women's Right to Speak   33

2. Women Preachers in the West   38
    Lucy Pierce Knott   43
    Maye McReynolds   50
    Santos Elizondo   53
    Elsie Wallace   62

3. Women Preachers in the Northeast   69
    Susan Norris Fitkin   72
    Martha E. Curry   83
    Olive M. Winchester   91

4. Women Preachers in the South 99
Mary Lee Harris Cagle 104
Elliott J. Sheeks 114

5. Women Preachers in the Southeast 122
Frances Rye McClurkan 126
Leila Owen Stratton 130
Leona Gardner 132

6. What It Takes for Women Ministers to Survive and Thrive 139
What Do the Lives of the First Generation
of Ordained Women Reveal? 139
What Happened to the Role of Ordained Women
During the Lifetimes of These Women? 143
What Discouraged Later Women
from Becoming Ministers? 144
What Does This Mean for Women Called
to the Ordained Ministry Today? 147

Notes 155

Bibliography 164

Recommended Reading 167

ACKNOWLEDGMENTS

Many people assisted me as I wrote this manuscript. Dr. Barbara Brown Zikmund, my seminary adviser at the Pacific School of Religion, first introduced me to the unheralded contributions of women in American Protestantism. She, Dr. Edwina Hunter, and Bishop Leontine T. C. Kelly provided living role models of ordained women committed to the church and to social justice that made my historical work come alive.

Dr. R. Stanley Ingersol, archivist of the Church of the Nazarene, directed me to the appropriate source materials in the archival holdings found at the International Headquarters of the Church of the Nazarene in Kansas City. Dialogues with Dr. Ingersol and insights gained from his dissertation, *Burden of Dissent: Mary Lee Cagle and the Southern Holiness Movement,* helped clarify and hone my initial zealous plans for this work. Brad Estep and Lon Dagley also shared their knowledge and cheerfully copied untold documents for my later use.

To aid in my own study, Dr. Janet Smith Williams, ordained elder and former professor of homiletics at the Nazarene Bible College in Colorado Springs, was willing to share her research on some of these Nazarene women and more recent statistical data and interviews on modern trends in women's ordained ministry.

Dr. Irving and Beverly Laird, my parents, paid numerous phone bills as they called to encourage me.

Rev. Michael Christensen, my husband, coached me through the research for this book as the delivery of our first daughter drew near. His confidence propelled me onward when it was debatable which "baby" would be delivered first.

Some of Our Best Men Are Women

From its earliest days, the Church of the Nazarene has officially recognized the ministerial rights of women. An oft-repeated folklore tells us that Phineas Bresee, one of the main denominational founders, was fond of saying, "Some of our best 'men' are women!"

The 1898 Constitution of the Los Angeles Church of the Nazarene, the "mother church," registered the same stance when it stated: "We recognize the equal right of both men and women to all offices of the Church of the Nazarene, including the ministry."[1]

The Church of the Nazarene traces many of its significant origins to 1895 in Los Angeles with the emergence of Los Angeles First Church, a local congregation that spawned others in the West and eventually led to a merger between the New England-centered Association of Pentecostal Churches and the West Coast Nazarenes. In 1907 the two independent groups moved toward becoming a national denomination. One year later in Pilot Point, Tex., the addition of preexisting holiness organizations in the South formally created a denomination that reached from East to West and North to South in the United States. Then in 1915 the Pentecostal Mission based in Nashville joined them and infused the young denomination with a strong foreign missionary focus.

Women's Ministry
in the Church of the Nazarene

Each of the regional holiness groups that merged in the early 1900s relied heavily on the service and leadership of women. Three of the four regional groups ordained women to the preaching ministry prior to joining forces to form a national denomination. The fourth group, the Pentecostal Mission, stalled in joining them for seven years, and the ordination of women was one of the main ideological differences. It is important to add, however, that the firm stance against ordaining women held by J. O. McClurkan, the founder of the Pentecostal Mission, did not keep them from serving as evangelists, missionaries, or teachers.[2]

McClurkan's objection was not to women preaching or having a public ministry; rather, he determined that the ordination of women for "ruling positions" was unscriptural.[3] However, McClurkan's position did not prevail after his death, and his wife, Frances Rye McClurkan, was ordained six years later.

Where Are the Women Preachers Now?

Today, the Church of the Nazarene proudly and appropriately claims its heritage of vigorous leadership by women in the ordained ministry. However, the influence of ordained women has decreased markedly over the years. Later generations have not renewed the church's historic legacy of women vigorously entering the ordained ministry. As a result, many people associated with the Church of the Nazarene are beginning to ask why proportionately fewer women presently serve the church as active ordained elders.

I personally began to ask, "Where are the women

preachers now?" after I graduated from college and began to think more seriously about my own call to the ministry. I looked around for role models and found few. I knew that women *could* serve the church in any capacity. Yet they weren't. I needed to see other women preach, teach theology, and serve as church leaders to confidently pursue my own path in ministry.

My search eventually led me to choose to attend a seminary where one-third of the faculty were female. This seminary had a woman dean—a strong church historian who introduced me to the hidden history of women in American Protestantism. The power of her example, along with that of my women professors, gave me courage and new skills for ministry. My three committee members were all ordained ministers—Congregational, United Methodist, and American Baptist. Yet I was a Nazarene. Where were the role models in my own tradition?

My search for material on early Nazarene women ministers was poorly rewarded until it led me to some century-old documents in the Nazarene archives. Little by little, I uncovered bits and pieces of information that introduced me to 12 of the earliest women preachers in the denomination. These women, who served the church nearly 100 years ago, became the role models I lacked during my formative years.

Changing Cultural Beliefs

As I met these foremothers through my research, I wondered what beliefs, actions, and social realities made it possible for them to play such important and vital roles in the earliest years of the Church of the Nazarene.

While no definitive answers are to be had, history provides a glimpse into the social, theological, and institutional climate that these women found favorable to their efforts in church leadership. The early women ordained in the Church of the Nazarene gained access to the pulpit based on an argument grounded in the doctrine of the Holy Spirit. Several held a dispensational view of the Holy Spirit, understanding that in special periods of history unusual gifts and freedoms are given by the Holy Spirit. One of the main biblical cornerstones on which these women built ministerial careers was the words of Joel quoted by Peter at Pentecost: "And in the last days it shall be, God declares, that I will pour out my Spirit upon all flesh, . . . and your daughters shall prophesy" (Acts 2:17, RSV).

The holiness movement that gave rise to the Church of the Nazarene understood the stirring of the Holy Spirit to be the most perceptible of spiritual actions. How, then, could women who testified to a clear calling of the Holy Spirit and who manifested obvious gifts be denied the right to preach? As women began publicly to exhort, first before women in prayer bands or meetings, then in mixed groups, ordination became the next step. The biblical mandate of Pentecost, along with the proven competence of the women who preached within the loosely structured holiness organizations, led to ordination. Ordination was both a bonus for faithful service and a seal of the church. However, as the church has grown, administrative structures and ordination requirements, combined with a steadily growing fundamentalist ideology, have increasingly deterred women from the preaching ministry and have effectively cut the numbers of women seeking ordination. While no policy change has occurred, a much smaller percentage of women were ordained after 1950 than in the denomination's first four decades.

Before 1950 the early Nazarene women ministers inherited the good done by the secular women's movement of the 19th century that arose in good measure from the churches and led to women gaining access to the pulpit and eventually acquiring the right to vote. Paradoxically, the "second wave" of the women's liberation movement of the 1960s and 1970s seems to have curtailed women's active leadership in the Church of the Nazarene. The radical feminist call for equality produced a backlash that led some to believe that redefining a Christian woman's primary place of influence as the home is the only way to maintain family strength.

Meanwhile a generation of young, aspiring Nazarene women have been raised in a society that has more opportunities than ever for career-minded women. Those of us raised within the Church of the Nazarene have been proudly told that the denomination has always ordained women. We find no historical or theological restraints to entering the ministry, yet there often is an invisible, barbed barrier that hinders the success of women in the ordained ministry.

I have labeled this obstacle as "negative affirmation." The denomination officially maintains a position that allows for the ordination of women, yet there has been little denominational support for women in the ministry. Many local congregations, perhaps most, do not consider calling a woman to serve as pastor when vacancies arise. Cultural prejudice, combined with prior experience with only male ministers, causes many churches to seek out the best *man* for the job. Without female role models and denominational support, it is no wonder that few women succeed in being ordained and in finding placement in a profession presently dominated by men.

This cultural barrier to women's ordination is further indicated by the fact that the denomination has rarely elected women to noticeable policy-making positions in the denomination outside traditional areas deemed fit for female involvement: world missions, children's ministries, and music. In effect, the 19th-century ideal of a "separate sphere"[4] that puts a priority on women's work at home or among the young or impoverished seems to have been institutionalized.

The Nazarene foremothers highlighted in the following chapters, however, chose not to live passively within a separate sphere. They crossed boundaries again and again and have left an inspiring legacy from which contemporary women seeking ordination can benefit. While the struggles of these 19th-century women differ significantly from our late-20th-century problems, learning more about their lives provides a starting point from which modern women can evaluate the foundation of women's ordained ministry. We can also be prompted to action by their courageous examples.

Most of the early Nazarene women preachers are more aptly described as spiritual activists rather than as feminists. They acted against cultural norms, but few verbally challenged male authority. Although the women preachers in the early Church of the Nazarene most certainly faced some vehement opposition, they showed little impulse to question or abandon the ideology of "separate spheres" of responsibility, even while living outside of it.

While these wonderfully vital women preached and agitated against alcohol, prostitution, and other social ills that had a personal, moral dimension, they rarely needed to tackle the daunting ills of institutional prejudice and the unspoken barriers that now exist in the Church of the Nazarene. Quite the opposite, the regional groups that merged to form the Church of the Nazarene provided an organizational flexibility and an obvious need for gifted workers of either sex that gave these women a place to serve.

The Church of the Nazarene began as a progressive, reformist group intent on being "a church of the people and for the people . . . not a mission, but a church with a mission."[5] The initial mission was to proclaim a deeper experience of God to all people and classes. Today proclaiming the holiness doctrine is often directly equated with conservative, family-oriented values that affirm women most when they work at home or help further their husbands' careers. For women in the late 20th century, the majority of whom are employed outside the home, this equation of holiness with the separate sphere ideology sends an insidious message that pursuing a vocation or calling is less important than being at home.

The woman who determines to seek ordination in the Church of the Nazarene must overcome the cultural biases that would keep her at home, especially if she is married with children. Even the church's recognition of a woman's right to preach as being grounded in the doctrine of the Holy Spirit, while helping to create policies that affirm women's rights to ordination, does little to uproot deeply held reservations about women in ministry.

As a result, many end up believing the false notion that a woman who is Spirit-led, gifted, and educated will surely flourish in ministry. Instead she may never be called to serve a congregation, which is one of the prerequisites for ordination.

The congregational polity and limited superintendency of the Church of the Nazarene has created another perplexing dilemma. Some women seminarians report being told informally by some district superintendents that churches on their districts will not accept women; accordingly, women's names and résumés are rarely submitted to churches with vacancies. This leaves the grassroots of the church without the vital female role models needed to help churches consider qualified women for all ministry positions.

So it seems that the agreement among the holiness movement that the Holy Spirit may be poured out upon women, thus enabling them to preach, is not enough to guarantee them that opportunity. What can be done to reawaken the Church of the Nazarene to the gift of women for the ordained ministry?

The lives of the 12 women preachers highlighted in this book offer some clues. Their lives show that an inclination to preach begins with the experience of a divine call—these holiness women clearly felt called to preach. But they didn't stop there. They underwent a conversion in ideology as to what they could do with their lives. They came to believe that they must preach despite the prevailing cultural attitudes. Then they acted against the prevailing attitudes toward women. They did what women were not expected to do—they preached, taught, and planted churches. And their actions challenged the validity of defining a woman's place by her gender rather than by her gifts and calling.

By examining the lives of these women, it can be shown that they served greatly in shaping the denomination precisely because they were convicted by the Holy Spirit to preach; they experienced a conversion as to what was appropriate to a woman's role in the church, and they acted upon their heartfelt beliefs whether or not supported by the church.

It is my hope that, in bringing to light the lives of these women, a resurgence of women's leadership in the Church of the Nazarene will take place. But such a movement will require several actions by the women who are called to preach. First, each woman must gird herself with a sound, scriptural defense of women's rights to all leadership roles. She will have to confront others who hold opposing views. Second, women ministers must dedicate themselves to speaking out whenever a woman's right to all leadership roles is threatened or ignored. When a church leader prays for all the "brothers in the ministry," that leader needs to be reminded that sisters are in the ministry too. Third, women ministers, along with denominational leaders, must be willing to find ways to consciously and frequently raise the question of women in ministry with local congregations. With a congregational polity, the laity must be asked to examine the historical affirmations of the church. It must be repeated often that women traditionally have been and still should be fully considered for every role in the church from pastor to usher. Disqualifying women from church positions (or simply not recruiting them) because they are women is an untenable practice theologically and historically. Full conversion always requires conviction, a change of beliefs, and a commitment to action. Freeing the gifts of all of God's people, male or female, Jew or Greek, slave or free, is a task of the truly converted.

A Word of Explanation

The following chapter introduces the 19th-century holiness movement in which the 12 women ministers were sanctified and called to preach. Subsequent chapters introduce the 12 women ministers by the regional holiness groups they joined prior to the emergence of the denomination known as the Church of the Nazarene.

Additionally, a word of explanation must be added as to why I've chosen to address the women by their first names, a practice these women did not employ. In the course of their lives, most of them changed their surnames at least once. Only first names remain constant. For example, one of the women was known as Mary Lee Wasson, Mary Lee Harris, and Mary Lee Cagle. Additionally, in source materials, the women are often referred to by their husbands' names, such as in the case of Mrs. DeLance Wallace, or simply Sister Wallace. I have chosen to call her Elsie Wallace. Using first names provides clarity when reading and also highlights the individuality and personal achievements of each woman.

Ordained Women in the Church of the Nazarene

1

The Changing Role
of Women
in the 19th Century

The ministry of women is one of the fascinating themes of the 19th-century holiness movement. While women have always served the church, it was during the 19th century that the question of women's ordination became an issue that denominations had to face. What happened to bring this concern to the attention of holiness churches? What enabled these women to take on roles that had previously been closed to them? What social, historical, and theological realities gave rise to the expanding role of women in the religious world? The answers to these questions will be briefly summarized before two prominent women in the mid-19th-century holiness movement—Antoinette Brown Blackwell and Phoebe Palmer—and their specific contributions to the public ministry of women are discussed.

The Changing Society
of the 19th Century

By the late 1840s great masses who were not predisposed to the fervent ways of American Protestantism immigrated into the United States, creating a national pluralism that had not previously existed.[1]

At the same time, the characteristically rural population of the nation began migrating to the cities. The early part of the century was an era of transition from agrarian to industrial capitalism. Industrialization replaced the self-contained farm as the norm for production. The masses of the immigrant poor, along with the newly urbanized workers, produced a large population in need of social aid. This group also was ripe for evangelization by the growing numbers of American revivalists who believed that a Christian citizenry was the key to a strong, democratic nation.

As social issues, such as workers' rights, slum conditions, racial distrust, and the liquor traffic moved to the fore of religious consciousness, crusades for the rights of oppressed groups became part of the religious agenda of the holiness movement.

The Separate Sphere Doctrine

During this same period the division of labor became increasingly stereotyped by gender. As more men worked in a locale other than the home-based farm, women primarily became associated with domestic life. Even for the many families still involved in farming, increased mechanization and productivity separated the work spheres.

The separate sphere ideology defined a woman's cultural place as tending the hearth and children while the men of the family fought the battles, pioneered the West, and developed the economy. Women were not necessarily considered inferior, only different. They were thought to possess a nature inherently more gentle and nurturing, while it was inborn in men to provide leadership in the rough-and-tumble world of politics and labor. Contemporary media, primarily through periodicals and advertisements, heralded the domestication of the American woman as the norm and as the highest attainment of the female sex.

As the woman's place was being defined, the home front itself was changing. Automated spinning jennies manufactured cloth, an innovation that usurped the need for each household to produce homespun on a spinning wheel. This and other new ways of manufacturing gave women, especially young women, the time to consider unprecedented possibilities and to forge new identities.

The Women's Movement of the 19th Century

The separate sphere doctrine, however pervasive, only camouflaged the practical variation in women's lives. Norms as to women's activities were more likely defined by economic class and ethnic origin than exclusively by gender. Many women, especially the newly migrated and immigrated, worked prior to marriage. Others, mainly from the middle classes, procured a place on the boundaries of the woman's sphere through reform and charitable activities. Many opted for greater involvement through service-related religious activities, yet only in the groups considered unorthodox, such as the Society of Friends, did women regularly speak or preach publicly.

As women joined the struggle against social ills, many became vocal against slavery. In raising their voices on behalf of their black brothers and sisters, these women themselves became the object of controversy. How dare they speak publicly? Weren't women to keep silent and stay at home?

Sarah and Angelina Grimke, Quaker sisters, were forced to defend their rights as women to speak out against slavery. Angelina, the younger, published a tract in 1836, *An Appeal to the Christian Women of the South*, that attracted much attention and resulted in the invitation to give a series of lectures for the American Antislavery Society. Angelina spoke out of her conviction that women, as well as blacks, were divinely created with inalienable rights. So compelling were her lectures that men soon started to attend the meetings of the women's society.

The collective clergy of the region were outraged at the idea of a woman speaking before a "promiscuous" (mixed gender) audience. Their attacks on Angelina aroused her loyal sister's ire. Sarah wrote and published *Letters on the Equality of the Sexes and the Condition of Women,* in which she vehemently argued for a woman's right to speak out as a full participant in society: "I ask no favors of my sex. I surrender not our claim to equality. All I ask of our brethren is that they will take their feet from off our necks, and permit us to stand upright on the ground which God has designed us to occupy."[2]

This philosophical "feminist" perspective was first publicly revealed and documented in the Declaration of Sentiments and Resolutions passed by the women who gathered in a Free Methodist church in Seneca Falls, N.Y., in 1848. This meeting heralded the first organized gathering of women committed to equal rights.

The early feminists called for equal pay, equal opportunity to work, and suffrage—the right to vote, demands that were not directly seen by all involved to contradict the notion of a woman's place. Many felt a woman could remain primarily committed to home and hearth while engaging in work prior to childbirth, and in professions in line with her innate role as moral guardian. Most of the first generation of ordained women in the Church of the Nazarene lived within the boundaries of this premise.

Amid this time of urbanization and debate on women's roles, the American holiness movement gained momentum and began to spread throughout the land.

The American Holiness Movement

The 19th-century holiness movement traced its theological and methodological roots to the reforms of John Wesley in the previous century.

Wesley, the founder of Methodism, taught that the purpose of Christianity was to restore sinful people to holiness of heart and life. The first step was to repent and believe that Jesus Christ's death atoned for sin. Wesley then encouraged a second step because he observed that people, although saved, continued to have diseased souls that were the inheritance of the Fall. This "second blessing" allowed the Holy Spirit to purify the heart by removing the inclination toward sinning. Wesley's theology became a goad that led to spiritual, ecclesiastical, and social reform in England.

John Wesley's mother, Susanna, encouraged her son to allow laymen to preach, advice that, when combined with Susanna's own success at turning her family worship time into a prayer meeting regularly attended by 200 people, later led to the partial acceptance of the preaching of lay women.

Wesley, however, even a decade after the initiation of Methodism, denied women the right to preach. He conceded that women could prophesy but that preaching and prophesying were different. It was only when some of the prayer bands, like Sarah Crosby's, grew to several hundred, prohibiting Sarah from speaking to each attender individually, that Wesley advised that she keep her exhortations short and "keep as far from what is called preaching as you can."[3]

Wesley's opinion later shifted. He newly reasoned that the movement of God through Methodism was so unusual that the old mores could be lifted. Wesley "remarked that even in Corinth where women were not permitted to speak, Paul made exceptions for the women who prophesied. In the same way, God's obvious but 'extraordinary' call of women to preach forced Wesley to make exceptions to the normal church rules."[4] After Wesley's change of heart, a continual stream of Methodist women took on the role of exhorter.[5]

As the holiness movement later gained momentum in the United States during the 19th century, a flurry of organizations or "unions" sprang up prior to the Civil War. Believers in the "higher life" could be found in denominations as divergent as the Baptists and Quakers. Weekday prayer meetings and national camp meetings boasted of their interdenominational characters.

As the popularity of holiness revivalism grew, so did the discomfort of portions of the established denominations. The independence and dissension that often racked the holiness associations gave many Methodist leaders pause.

This growing rift within Methodism spurred some independent holiness groups onward, and the holiness movement became increasingly equated with dissenting, independent groups. Many faithful lay people remained members of both a denomination and a local holiness association. Over time, however, the call for loyalty from both sides created great tension because only a core of shared beliefs kept the holiness groups aligned.

Theological Beliefs of the Holiness Movement

The theological threads that tied together these holiness organizations are all rooted in the experiential nature of the doctrine of Christian perfection.

Public Testimony

A common requirement for membership in a holiness group was giving testimony to sanctification or claiming to be a seeker after the holiness experience. This bottom line of experience led to an emphasis on spiritual egalitarianism or the "priesthood of all believers." What did it matter if one was ordained or not if the essential credential of sanctification was the confirmation of the Spirit in one's life? Giving public testimony of the work of the Holy Spirit was understood as a better indicator of spirituality than certificates or diplomas.

This experiential focus was a main factor in the gradual acceptance of women speaking in mixed public groups. A well-known story from the life of Phoebe Palmer, who was perhaps the most influential woman in the holiness movement, illustrates how this mandate to give witness to the work of the Holy Spirit challenged the widely held bias against women speaking.

A woman attending one of Palmer's Tuesday Meetings for the Promotion of Holiness in New York City stood to share her sincere desire to be sanctified. The woman, however, was in a quandary; she knew "one of the conditions for receiving the blessing was to speak as the Spirit gave her utterance. But the church she attended forbade women to speak. What should she do when the will of Christ and the will of the church were in conflict?"[6]

Phoebe addressed the question of a woman's obligation to speak by gleaning from Scripture and appealing to a higher loyalty. She argued, "When any human organization, even the church, conflicts with Christ, one must obey God rather than man."[7]

Emphasis on the Second Coming

The holiness movement also inherited the optimism characteristic of the many theories on the second coming of Christ that pervaded the 19th century. The belief that the kingdom of God was soon to become reality on earth was rampant. However, opinions of when and how the reign of

Christ would take place were regularly disputed. Heightened last-day expectations tend to lead to a more flexible interpretation of ecclesiastical roles because if one believes that Christ is returning soon, what matters is getting ready, not who is doing the preaching. So it is no coincidence that intensified focus on the Second Coming and increased opportunities for women in the church occurred simultaneously.

Compassionate Ministry and Moral Reform

Some holiness groups focused their attention on Christ's imminent return. Other holiness revivalists like Charles Grandison Finney stressed holiness as a movement that would transform the present world. By the time the Pentecostal Church of the Nazarene emerged, theological debate centered less on how the holiness movement would transform society and more on how individuals could be saved from moral ruin. Many rescue missions were established to save the individual from sin and degradation.

The Church of the Nazarene began during the latter years of the 19th century in southern California out of a desire to evangelize the poor. Dr. Bresee believed that offering a rescue mission to the poor was not enough. They, too, were to be full members of the church with all rights and responsibilities. This compassionate focus on reaching the "neglected quarters" was also a theological characteristic of the holiness movement, and it became the mandate of the early Church of the Nazarene. This focus on bringing the church to the poor was a burden the first generation of ordained women would shoulder with great earnestness.

Many factors, social, historical, and theological, converged in the 19th century to open the way for women to speak publicly. Once women began to find acceptance, albeit limited, to their public ministry, seeking ordination was the next step out of the centuries of silence.

Antoinette Brown Blackwell and Women's Ordination

Revivalism flourished throughout the 19th century. Tent meetings and special services abounded. One of the most influential preachers, Charles Grandison Finney, trooped up and down the eastern part of the country gathering great crowds and stressing that "intellectual talent and training should be devoted to the dual work of saving souls and transforming society."[8]

Finney would later serve as professor of theology at Oberlin College in Ohio, noted for its coeducational training of both blacks and whites. The holiness strain associated with Oberlin gave the theory of Christian perfection a broad focus. Oberlin staunchly held an abolitionist position and also became a gathering place for women desiring to expand their minds and activities. Sanctification, rather than being an experience of divine cleansing from inbred sin, was interpreted as a consecration that could be easily wedded to the social reform platform.

The Joseph and Abigail Brown family was highly influenced by Finney's preaching in Rochester, N.Y., during an 1831 revival. As a result, their daughter, Antoinette Brown Blackwell, would become the first ordained woman in America. In her teens, Antoinette experienced a call to preach and formulated the ambition to become a minister. Then in 1846 she traveled to Oberlin College to obtain an education in preparation for her public work. She would later return to Oberlin to take up theological studies despite strong opposition for Oberlin, while committed to a woman's right to general education, balked at offering theological training to women. Antoinette and another female student, Lettice Smith, were allowed to sit in on courses and do the academic work, but "were 'excused' from participation in discussion, debates, or rhetorical exhibitions.

They learned to write; men learned to write *and to speak* . . .
Public speaking was considered unseemly for proper
young ladies."[9]

This did not stop Antoinette, Lettice, and a few other
women classmates, however. They revived a defunct liter-
ary society in order to teach themselves to speak publicly,
and they convinced a professor to allow them to stage a
debate in class. Their successful debate produced vigorous
protests from the faculty and the Ladies Board, the governing agency for women students. Antoinette Brown and
Lettice Smith graduated but were not listed among the theological students in the class of 1850 until 1908.

Brown traveled and lectured for the next three years
until a church in South Butler, N.Y., invited her in 1853 to
become its pastor. The church was small and poor, but Antoinette served the church so well that by the summer, the
governing board determined to publicly recognize her
ministry by conferring ordination. According to Congregational polity, the local church has the authority to call and
ordain its own minister without additional denominational
approval. Therefore on September 15, 1853, Rev. Luther
Lee, a founder and theologian in the abolitionist Wesleyan
Methodist Connection, preached Antoinette Brown's ordination sermon from Gal. 3:28, emphasizing that in Christ
there is no male nor female. Lee's remarks summarized his
view of the meaning of ordination and why women were
duly qualified:

> I do not believe that any special or specific form of or-
> dination is necessary to constitute a gospel minister. We are
> not here to make a minister. It is not ours to confer on this
> our sister a right to preach the gospel. If she has not that
> right already, we have no power to communicate it to her.
> Nor have we met to qualify her for the work of the min-
> istry. If God and mental and moral culture have not already
> qualified her, we cannot, by anything we may do by way of
> ordaining or setting her apart. . . . All we are here to do, and

all we expect to do, is, in due form, and by a solemn and impressive service, to subscribe our testimony to the fact that in our belief, our sister in Christ, Antoinette L. Brown, is one of the ministers of the New Covenant, authorized, qualified, and called of God to preach the gospel of his Son Jesus Christ.[10]

Less than a year after her ordination, the pressures, doubts, and isolation of her position led Antoinette to resign her pastorate and return to her family's farm for recuperation.

Later, after Antoinette regained her health, she continued in public work—preaching, lecturing, and writing on women's rights and the spiritual life. In January 1856 she married Samuel Blackwell of a strong abolitionist family, and together they had seven children, two of whom did not survive infancy.

Phoebe Palmer and Women's Right to Speak

Phoebe Worrall Palmer was born December 18, 1807, in New York City to parents committed to Methodism. Her life embodies, perhaps as none other, the zeal and influence of women's participation in the holiness movement. Unlike Antoinette Brown Blackwell, who agitated for women's rights and social transformation, Phoebe was mainly interested in evangelistic efforts that led to spiritual conversion. Phoebe was a lay theologian, a writer, a sought-after revival speaker, a tireless reformer, and an advocate of women's empowerment by the Holy Spirit for ministry.

As the holiness movement crossed the Atlantic from England and moved through American Methodism, Phoebe Palmer became its best-known proponent in America, and later her esteem was extended to England through her various preaching tours.

In 1833 Phoebe and her husband, Walter, lost the third

of their six children to an early death. That same year they attended the Allen Street Methodist Episcopal Church and went forward to kneel and dedicate themselves to the work of "spiritual holiness." The proximity of this spiritual act to the death of their child amply suggests that Phoebe interpreted the death of her child as God's way of calling her to a life that required more of her than motherhood.

In her journal, Phoebe elaborates: "I have often felt as though God had called me peculiarly to a life of holiness. I have also felt that in order to be led in this way, the path of self-denial must be mine. . . . Rather let me tread onward in the footsteps of Him who was a 'man of sorrows and acquainted with grief.'"[11]

She comforted her questioning mind in the face of sorrow by trusting that God would only call her into constructive, holy endeavors. She continued in this way, dedicated to holiness even when she had not yet experienced the Holy Spirit's outpouring as a confirmation of sanctification as had her husband, Walter. In spite of this, Phoebe and her sister, Sarah Lankford, instituted a weekly afternoon prayer meeting that would later come to be known as the "Tuesday Meeting for the Promotion of Holiness." Finally, after years of seeking, Phoebe came to full confirmation of her sanctification on July 26, 1837.

Phoebe's own experience of sanctification influenced her theology throughout the remainder of her life. Hers was not an experience confirmed with great emotion. Rather, the conditions that Phoebe came to view as necessary to claim sanctification were, first, to lay one's all on the altar [which was Christ]. Second, one had to "resolve to enter into an internal covenant with the Lord, and finally, one had to believe that the offering of one's will and life would be acceptable in God's sight."[12]

She believed fervently that holiness was not to be the possession of a few, but was rather a "state of grace in which every one of the Lord's redeemed should live."[13] Sanctification wasn't the culmination of the Christian life, but the beginning of it.

Taking on the task of proclaiming holiness to "every one of the Lord's redeemed" led Phoebe to an active, public ministry. In the years following her commitment and sanctification, Phoebe served for 11 years as secretary for the New York Female Assistance Society for the Relief and Religious Instruction of the Sick Poor; founded the Five Points Mission, an institution with a chapel, schoolroom, baths, and 25 rent-free apartments for the indigent; traveled across the eastern parts of the United States, Canada, and throughout the British Isles preaching in partnership with her husband; wrote eight books; and edited a periodical, *Guide to Holiness.* Additionally, she distributed tracts in the New York slums, organized a mission in China that her husband financed almost single-handedly from his medical practice, and attempted to launch an outreach to the Jewish population in New York City. These activities were a direct response to Phoebe's sense of calling, and a call to preach was certainly part of her life: "That God has called me to stand before the people, and proclaim His truth, has long been beyond question. So fully has God made my commission known to my own soul . . . [through] the conversion of thousands of precious souls, and the sanctification of a multitude of believers, that even Satan does not seem to question that my call is divine."[14]

Phoebe never sought nor did she receive any formal preaching license; she felt it unnecessary. She maintained that the whole structure of an ordained clergy was absurd. It was Phoebe's observation that more people came to a deepened spiritual experience through hearing lay testimonies than through sermons and that no one who had experienced sanctification had the right to remain silent when God prompted. So she preached, powerfully and often, despite hardship and criticism. Her language describing sanctification (such as "laying one's all on the altar") was often the target of unkind labels. She was called "un-Wesleyan" and "un-Methodist"! Neither was she exempt from the judgments of those who felt women were scripturally prohibited to preach or speak publicly.

In 1872 Phoebe addressed these concerns in her book *Promise of the Father*. The title accurately focused Phoebe's argument. Throughout she refers to two specific scriptural references:

> And it shall come to pass afterward, that I will pour out my spirit upon all flesh; and your sons and your daughters shall prophesy *(Joel 2:28)*.

> And, behold, I send the promise of my Father upon you but tarry ye in the city of Jerusalem, until ye be endued with power from on high *(Luke 24:49)*.

These verses formed the basis of her conviction that women were free to preach.

Phoebe believed that the Christian Church had lapsed from scriptural truth by silencing women. She boldly proclaimed, "The church in many ways is a sort of potter's field, where the gifts of women, as so many strangers, are buried. How long, O Lord, how long before man shall roll away the stone that we may see a resurrection?"[15]

Her allusion to "resurrection" was intentional. Another of her other passionate defenses of woman's place in the church is the biting poem about Mary, who was the first to tell the good news of Christ's resurrection:

> *Not she with traitorous kiss her Savior*
> *Not she denied him with unholy tongue:*
> *She, while apostles shrank, could danger brave,*
> *Last at his cross, first at his grave.*[16]

Again and again Phoebe's pointed remarks and prodding show a strong defense of women's public ministry. Part of

Phoebe's intent for writing *Promise of the Father* was to urge ministers to pray about how they viewed women. When they saw the error of their previous prejudices, they were to instruct their churches in seeing women as coheirs of God's gifts.

Beyond this type of agitation in behalf of the freedom of sanctified women to publicly say so, Phoebe never fully espoused the broader women's rights movement. She hedged on the subject: "We believe woman has her legitimate sphere of action, which differs in most cases material from that of man; and in this legitimate sphere she is both happy and useful. Yet we don't doubt that some reforms contemplated in recent movements may in various respects, be decidedly advantageous."[17]

Phoebe felt passionately that God's gifts were never to be ignored or silenced regardless of the sex of the believer, but she also maintained that women were normally to be "helpmeets" for their spouses. Yet in fulfilling her role as helpmeet to her husband, she preached to tens of thousands worldwide.

Antoinette and Phoebe laid, with the mortar of their lives, the first stepping-stones that later Nazarene women ministers would tread as they continued to pioneer the way for women in the ministry.

2

Women Preachers
in the West

As women slowly gained access to the pulpit, the holiness movement experienced growth, but at the same time, greater separation came between the established denominations and independent holiness associations. The first regional group to call itself the Church of the Nazarene emerged amid these tensions.

Phineas F. Bresee and the Church of the Nazarene in the West

Phineas F. Bresee, born in 1838 to Methodist parents in western New York state, would later be viewed as the primary founder of the Church of the Nazarene. Bresee experienced conversion by the age of 17 and soon received an exhorter's license in New York. He entered the ministry after his family moved to a prairie homestead in Iowa. By 1861 he had served two years as a minister in "full connection" and was ordained as a Methodist elder. The open terrain of Iowa honed the young preacher's skills as he fulfilled the responsibilities of a circuit rider. Even during his early years as a minister he began to use popular choruses in worship services and to train the laity to provide prayerful assistance to seekers at the altar—characteristics that, one day, would become well-known traits of the Church of the Nazarene.

Sometime during the winter of 1866-67, Bresee experienced an inner shift in his spirituality. The young minister had been plagued with doubts and wondered if his youthful entrance into the ministry had kept him from thoroughly answering the deep questions of faith. After much study, Bresee spent a tearful time of prayer at the altar of his church in Chariton, Iowa. He did not knowingly pray for the experience of sanctification, as he had not yet become acquainted with the holiness doctrine. Historian Timothy Smith recounts what Bresee later recorded about that day: "'But in my ignorance, the Lord helped me, and gave me, as I believe, the baptism with the Holy Ghost. Though I did not know either what I needed or what I prayed for.' He remembered that the experience took away his tendencies to 'worldliness, anger and pride,' and removed the doubt as well."[1]

Bresee successfully served as pastor of churches in Iowa for the next 16 years and served as presiding elder and a delegate to the General Conference in 1876. He prospered materially as well until 1883 when an ill-fated gold mining venture in Mexico left him nearly bankrupt and sorely humiliated. Within months the large Bresee family, including seven children and two grandparents, was en route to Los Angeles. In spite of this episode, however, the Iowa conference later recognized Bresee's laudable service. His financial trouble didn't seem to dampen their impression of him, yet he had already left Iowa before he knew that his reputation was untarnished.

Once the Bresee family arrived in southern California, Phineas was immediately asked to preach at the First Methodist Church of Los Angeles. Within two weeks he was installed as pastor. In this new charge, Phineas first encountered an influential group of laity who heartily professed and advocated the holiness doctrine and life.

Just months after Bresee's arrival a revival conducted by two leaders of the National Holiness Association in

1884, instilled in Bresee a renewed desire to pray privately for his own spiritual needs. His fervent prayer culminated as he saw a meteorlike ball of light, and he heard a sound that seemed to instruct him to eat and swallow the light. Bresee's account of the experience recalls:

> I swallowed only a little of it, although it felt like fire on my lips, and the burning sensation did not leave them for several days. While all of this itself would be nothing, there came with it into my heart and being, a transformed condition of life and blessing and unction and glory, which I had never known before . . . I was always very reticent in reference to my own personal experience. I have never gotten over it, and I have said very little relative to this; but there came into my ministry a new element of spiritual life and power.[2]

After this mystical encounter Bresee became a wholehearted believer in entire sanctification. During his three-year stay at the First Methodist Church of Los Angeles, Bresee built the membership to 650 members before accepting an appointment in Pasadena. After two years there, the congregation reportedly grew from 130 to more than 700 members, a phenomenon that led to the building of a huge, simple tabernacle—another act that Bresee would incorporate as a later Nazarene ideal; churches were to be built without pretense in locations that were accessible to many.

In addition to establishing a large church, Bresee began mission work among the Asian population and successfully worked to make Pasadena into California's first alcohol-free community. Due to his successes, in 1891 Bresee was appointed as presiding elder of the Los Angeles District and given the permission to organize holiness revivals throughout the next year.

Meanwhile, increased regional activity among independent holiness organizations combined with national outbreaks of fanaticism, began to concern some Methodist leaders. The appointment of Bishop John H. Vincent, an opponent of the holiness movement, as presiding elder of the Southern California Conference in 1892 led to the drawing up of battle lines between the Methodist groups in favor and those opposed to the holiness doctrine.

Vincent, who did not want holiness revivals taking place all over the Los Angeles area, quietly reappointed Bresee as the minister of a congregation that held a sure opposition to the holiness message and its concurrent social concerns. After several months Bresee knew he would not stay and requested an appointment as a city missionary. His request was denied, and he was reassigned to another church. His influence within southern California did not diminish during this period despite his theological conflicts with the bishop. Districts still sought him out as a camp meeting speaker, and he continued as he had since 1884, as a vice president of the board of directors of the University of Southern California (USC).

In 1884 Bresee and the president of USC, his longtime friend J. P. Widney, who was also a physician, felt they had placed the university on firm financial footing, and they accepted the invitation of Rev. and Mrs. T. P. Ferguson to assist them in the enlargement of Peniel Hall—a nondenominational mission with a goal to

> reach the unreached. The people from the homes and the street where the light from the churches does not reach, or penetrates but little. Especially to gather the poor to the cross, by bringing to bear upon them Christian sympathy and helpfulness . . .
>
> It is also our work to preach and teach the gospel of full salvation; to show forth the blessed privilege of believers in Jesus Christ, to be made holy and thus perfect in love.[3]

Dr. Bresee's request for another special assignment to Peniel Hall by his conference was denied. So after three days of prayerful seeking for guidance, Bresee asked for a "location," that is, a favorable discharge from his duties and responsibilities to the Methodist conference. Upon receiving it, he began to assist with the work at Peniel.

Services commenced in the newly completed hall which could seat up to 900 worshipers. A Tuesday holiness meeting, a noontime prayer gathering, a Sunday School program, and Friday night youth meeting soon made the work of Peniel Hall seem more like a local church than a rescue mission.

Within a few months, the differences arose between Bresee and the Fergusons, the founders of Peniel Hall. During the late summer of 1895 Bresee traveled to the Midwest to attend a series of National Holiness Association camp meetings. While there, new power structures were established at Peniel that left Bresee technically in charge yet stripped of authority. Upon his return to southern California, the proprietors soon asked him to leave.

Within weeks Bresee and J. P. Widney turned this unexpected series of events into an opportunity to establish a new church for the poor. They rented Red Men's Hall in downtown Los Angeles and publicized a service for October 6, 1895. The new denomination had no official name but Widney later came up with the name "Nazarene," which he claimed implied "the great toiling, struggling, sorrowing heart of the world. It is Jesus, Jesus of Nazareth, to whom the world in its misery and despair turns, that it may have hope."[4]

The new church was to be evangelistic in purpose, congregational in government, and identified with the poor. Bresee and Widney, both of whom had been associated with the Methodist form of government by bishops, chose a more democratic structure for the new denomination. Congregations could freely choose their own pastors and leaders.

This congregational form of government opened the way for women to lead in the early days of the denomination. Women like Lucy Knott and Maye McReynolds worked tirelessly alongside Bresee and other lay people to build satellite mission congregations throughout the city of Los Angeles. As the women were well-known to those who attended the mission services, it is not surprising that they naturally came to serve the groups as pastors. Theological degrees were not yet required; faithful service and evidence of giftedness were the only credentials needed.

Little detail is known of Bresee's view of women's ministry, yet his advocacy is clear. It is an oft-quoted folklore that Bresee was fond of saying about the women workers in the movement, "Some of our best men are women!" It is probable that Bresee knew of the ordination of Antoinette Brown. South Butler, N.Y., where she served as pastor, was less than 100 miles from his boyhood home. His abolitionist ties would have also acquainted him with the strong women speakers of the previous decades. He certainly knew of the work of Phoebe Palmer, and he also heard Amanda Berry Smith, a black evangelist, speak in southern California in 1891. He describes Amanda's proficient preaching on this occasion: "She preached one Sabbath afternoon, as I never heard her preach before, in strains of holy eloquence and unction . . . The Lord opened heaven on the people in mighty tides of glory."[5]

The fledgling Church of the Nazarene grew quickly. New converts worshiped alongside a small but influential group of former Methodists. Counted among this group were William S. Knott, a lawyer and judge, and his wife, Lucy Pierce Knott, one of the first women to be licensed and later ordained in the Church of the Nazarene in southern California.

Lucy Pierce Knott

Lucy Pierce was born on July 18, 1856, in Lancaster, Ky. Little is known of her early life until she married

William S. Knott on May 3, 1882. During the first years of
the Knotts' married life, Lucy gave birth to three children:
Thomas, Evelyn, and James Proctor. Only J. Proctor sur-
vived past infancy.

In 1887 the Knotts moved from Kentucky to Los Angeles, where they became acquainted with Phineas Bresee.
They later moved from church to church, as Bresee took
new appointments, until they joined the Church of the
Nazarene as charter members.

Lucy and her sister, Mrs. Baldwin, are described in the
words of Phineas Bresee as "Kentucky women of distin-
guished ability. Their early life was given to society and
worldliness. Although members of the Methodist church
for many years, they were not converted."[6] Lucy's obituary
in the denominational magazine cites the date of her conversion as 1892 and that of her sanctification as 1893.[7]

Lucy's sister, Mrs. Baldwin, helped found the Deets
Pacific Bible College in southern California and became
one of its first teachers. She is remembered as an intellectual and spiritual power who influenced her students
through teaching and the denomination by her prolific
writing.

Bresee's recorded memories of Lucy show that she
shared strong leadership skills with her sister:

> Mrs. Lucy P. Knott early became the leader of a some-
> what noted movement among the young women, [Compa-
> ny E] which led her into the wider field of a minister among
> us. In the early years of her work she became pastor of what
> was known as the Mateo Street mission, which was soon or-
> ganized into a church, and afterward came to be known as
> the Compton Avenue church. This has been one of the most
> successful churches of our denomination. It is now known
> as Emmanuel Church. Sister Knott has been especially inter-
> ested in the missionary work, both home and foreign, and
> her influence, together with the large offerings which her
> church has made, have been felt in many lands. As a preach-

er and leader in the church, she has shown peculiar ability. The Lord has greatly blessed her work, giving her a constant tide of salvation among all the classes, from little children to old people. She has always enjoyed the hearty co-operation of her husband, Judge W. S. Knott, who entered our movement with her, and thoroughly sympathizes with her in her work, himself preaching and teaching as occasion offers.[8]

As Bresee wrote, Lucy enjoyed the complete support of her husband. Her ministry began with young girls and then expanded. Perhaps the freedom and support she felt allowed her to fulfill her calling without completely changing her view of women's roles. In a letter written to H. F. Reynolds, general superintendent, regarding a woman missionary in Japan in 1913, Lucy revealed her position on women in leadership positions.

> For a long time I have seen the great necessity of having the right man at the head of things there. Not a word is to be said against women leaders in certain places and under certain conditions; but there *are* conditions where we must take a back seat, and depend upon our big brothers to do that, which we can not do. In each of our mission fields we should have a central mission, under the leadership of an experienced preacher and pastor.[9]

Lucy's own work began under the auspices of Bresee. And during most of her ministry she collaborated with her son, J. Proctor Knott, who also was ordained by the Nazarenes.

Lucy's earliest contribution was the organization of Company E, a group formed in 1898 out of a scheme that divided the church membership into alphabetical companies in order to promote small-group ministry endeavors. Lucy declared the name was taken from 1 Timothy 4:12: "Be thou an E—xample." Her words describe its purpose best:

> The object of this society is not so much that of evangelistic work in its regular meetings, but *primarily*, the study of the word, and for intercessory prayer. Equipped with the *doctrine*, and inspired with the vision that comes with fer-

vent prayer, sanctified young womanhood is a marvelous power in the church . . . Our daughters shall prophesy: and Company E is a training school in doctrine, service and practical personal holy living.[10]

Lucy agreed to lead the group with the stipulation that its membership could grow without limitation. At its zenith, Company E exceeded 250 members.

A license to preach was granted to Lucy in 1899 when she was 43 years old. Two years later, she took charge of the Mateo Street Mission when there was a membership of 10, including two children.[11] The February 12, 1903, *Nazarene Messenger* carries an account of the Sunday evening service where Lucy became fully ordained to the ministry:

> Dr. Bresee preached a short appropriate sermon; then five persons were received into the Church. The pastor, Mrs. Lucy P. Knott, was then set apart by ordination service to the office of an elder to which she had been elected. The service of her own covenant, the reading of the Scriptures, and ordination prayer were not only very impressive but in the solemn service there was evidently the presence of Him who alone sets apart and empowers His servants to minister to His glory. Then there was enjoyed the Sacrament of the Lord's supper.

Lucy had a strong interest in missions, so while serving at the Mateo Street Mission she instituted an envelope system for collecting missionary offerings. The system was built upon the slogan, "Something in the Envelope Every Month for Everybody." Before instituting the new system in 1902-3, Lucy's congregation raised $30.00 for missions. In 1904 they contributed $164.69. After the envelope system was begun in December 1904, the church raised $227.50 in the next year and $729.59 the following year while building, without debt, a church facility. Within a short time, the church building was moved to 38th and Compton Streets and the Mateo Street Mission became known as the Compton Avenue Church. Lucy's fund-raising technique caught the attention of the district treasurer who then asked if she would attend the 1907 General Assembly and present the system for raising missionary funds to the growing denomination.

Lucy's concern for missions went far beyond simply raising funds. Her letters to church leaders often advocated for those serving abroad who had been in direct contact with her. During 1912 the Compton Avenue Church raised money to build a mission house to shelter children at the Hope School in Calcutta.

From her writings it is clear that Lucy held a special concern for religious education of young people both at home and abroad. Her book-length works titled *Student's Bible Text Book, The Exalted Name, The Triune Name,* and *The Book of Revelation,* all share the focus of making the Bible doctrinally clear, prescriptive, and memorable for children and new converts.

In 1912, soon after the fund-raising effort for the Hope School, the Compton Church opened Emmanuel Private School for students in the first to ninth grades whose "parents are awake to the infidel and immoral atmosphere of the public schools." Lucy used *The Joyful Sound,* the church paper, to publicize the school, make announcements, give reports, and write poetry.

Lucy's church was noted as the second largest church on the district for many years. Dr. Bresee is quoted as saying, "This is a model church—a home, a training school, and a conquering army."

One little anecdote found in *The Joyful Sound* shows how Lucy was loved by her congregation. On the Friday before Christmas of 1910, she came home to find an elegant bookcase as a gift from the church. Lucy, reporting the event in the third person, wrote, "The intrinsic value of the gift was not the thing that melted her heart but the confidence and love it represented." Along with the bookcase, she was presented with a mounted copy of the following poem, which aptly shows her parishioners understood her commitment and followed her leadership:

Our Pastor

Who came to Mateo, in our great need,
When Satan prevailed, and our hearts did bleed,
Who labored and prayed, till she did succeed?
    Our Pastor.

Whose heart was filled with mission zeal,
And by prayer, and God's work did appeal
Till we've proved the joy of God's own seal?
    Our Pastor.

Who taught us in financial ways,
Showing us how God's money to raise
By "tithes and offerings" GIVING HIM PRAISE?
    Our Pastor.

Who planned those little envelopes grand,
With the angel announcing Christ's command
To preach the Gospel in every land?
    Our Pastor.

Who gave the P. N. Church our pin,
That we some passer-by might win,
And see him saved from pride and sin?
    Our Pastor.

Who tells us Jesus is coming again
To this poor world in peace to reign;
Eliminating all grief and pain?
    Our Pastor.

Who edits our little JOYFUL SOUND,
Which visits our neighborhood around,
Telling where our lighthouse may be found?
    Our Pastor.

Who needs our prayer and love to aid
In the many duties upon her laid?
(In Glory Land we'll all be paid.)
    Our Pastor.

Who needs this roomy bookcase, new,
For her many volumes old and true?
And those dear Promise Boxes, too?
    Our Pastor.
—With love inexpressible.
The Compton Avenue Church.[12]

Little is specifically known of her beliefs or style of ministry. Theologically she was an ardent premillennialist; she believed that Christ would return before the Tribulation. This was a theological position the denomination would not require of its members,[13] and this may be one explanation, although purely based on conjecture, as to why she and her ordained son, James Proctor, withdrew their credentials from the Nazarene denomination in 1920. In 1923 the two were received back from the Baptist church and are numbered among those organizing a new Nazarene church in Hollywood. The minutes record the event simply by saying,

> J. Proctor Knott spoke a few words of his appreciation of the Church of the Nazarene, and that he had experienced three years of homesickness. He told of the buying of a church site and of plans for their new church [presumably the Hollywood church]. Mrs. Lucy P. Knott spoke of her love for, and appreciation of the love of the Nazarenes. Dr. Goodwin [a general superintendent] spoke of the great, broad spirit of the Church of the Nazarene. The credentials

of Mrs. Lucy P. Knott and J. Proctor Knott were referred to the Committee on Orders and Relations for recognition and restoration.[14]

From 1923, when she reunited with the denomination, until 1940, Lucy served as associate pastor, with her son as pastor, of the Hollywood Church of the Nazarene. She died in 1940 just days shy of her 88th birthday.

Maye McReynolds

Maye was born in Green Lake County, Wis., and married Aaron McReynolds in Garden City, Minn., in 1874. In December 1883 when Maye was 29, they moved to Pasadena where Aaron opened the first general merchandise store in the area and became the local agent for the San Gabriel Valley Railroad. Maye took over the job when the transcontinental railroad was built. The McReynolds family included six children—five boys and one girl.

While visiting Los Angeles on business as a local agent for the Santa Fe Railroad in South Pasadena, Maye attended a revival where Phineas Bresee was preaching, and she experienced sanctification. She had been converted at the age of 12 and belonged to a Baptist church prior to her holiness experience, which occurred sometime in 1898 or early 1899.[15]

Maye soon joined the Church of the Nazarene and felt compelled to work among the Spanish-speaking people of Los Angeles that she encountered daily while working with the railroad. She became fluent in Spanish and preached and wrote it proficiently. Then she left her job with the railroad in 1903 and began visiting door to door among the Mexican people. Her church, recognizing her calling, supported her as a missionary to the Spanish-speaking Americans.

As her work grew, so did Maye's influence. She was

ordained in October 1906 as pastor of the Mexican mission
and later as pastor of the First Nazarene Mexican Church
of Los Angeles. Her efforts focused on meeting both spiritual and material needs. A sewing circle was established to
help those of Mexican heritage who needed clothing. In
her quarterly report of 1910, Maye wrote, "Clothing and
household goods have been distributed among the poor
and needy, regardless of denomination or creed. We have
thus been enabled to minister to their spiritual wants, and
many have thus been brought to Jesus."[16]

A remarkable account in the *Nazarene Messenger* of
June 18, 1908, shows her pastoral concern for souls and
that she was one to be involved in the lives of people who
may not have lived according to her own moral standards.
"I married a couple last week who had been living together for nearly two years, having procured the license in August, 1906. The woman was dying with consumption and
wanted a clear record. The dear Lord forgave her and afterward answered her heart cry for cleansing."[17]

From her earliest days as a minister, Maye showed
concern for the educational opportunities of those in her
church. By 1909 she was directing a class of 20 as they
studied language and Bible in Spanish. She hoped that the
Spanish educational work would become a branch of
Deets Pacific Bible College.

Maye McReynolds was a confident, bold woman with
great compassion. During the time when Pancho Villa held
the Southwest in a reign of terror, she sought to meet with
the bandit leader to plead for the welfare of her people.
She was received courteously by Pancho Villa in his boxcar
headquarters and left with promises of cooperation.

She also initiated the publication of the *Herald of Holiness* in Spanish and personally ministered to lay workers
throughout the Southwest. Her work reached ever south-
ward as converts began to take the gospel message into

New Mexico, Arizona, and the country of Mexico. By 1911 it was an established fact that Maye was the overseer of the work among the Spanish-speaking people. During the Third General Assembly of the Pentecostal Church of the Nazarene held in Nashville, the minutes recall that it was "moved and seconded that Sister McReynolds, who has been for years recognized as Superintendent of our Spanish Missions in the Southwestern part of the country, be recognized as a regular District Superintendent and seated in the assembly as such. Motion carried."[18]

The November 2, 1911, issue of the *Nazarene Messenger* boasts a picture of the general and district superintendents of the denomination. The diminutive Maye, dressed in black and white garb, stands as the lone female surrounded by 23 other denominational leaders. The picture is rare indeed as only one other woman, Elsie Wallace, has ever served in a district superintendency role.

Serving in this district leadership role was not easy. Some years later when the Mexican District was moving toward voting for its own leadership and it looked like Maye would be duly elected to continue the work she had done unofficially for years, she tells of resistance she experienced when assigned as the district leader before the vote:

> From the day that Bro Hampton heard of the action of the two Gen Supts, in making me Dist Supt, he immediately sent me his resignation and he and his spent two and a half months and money visiting the churches trying to stir up dissention [sic] with the result to them of the loss of the confidence of our people. As I have written to you before the churches have worked with me, evidently in perfect harmony, as evidenced by the presence and blessing of God in the Assembly.
>
> The enemy said "We cannot hope to gain, if the people are allowed to vote, so we will PREVAIL upon Bro. Reynolds to APPOINT instead of allowing them the right of

ballot, our people said if we are not allowed to vote, it does not look like liberty of thought or action."[19]

Perhaps the key to Maye's ministry is found later in this same letter, "One of my secrets of success with my people is not to oppose them in their desire UNLESS I am persuaded that they are in the wrong; I believe in them, and that they desire the right as they see it."[20]

Maye McReynolds is remembered as a radiant spirit and a devoted missionary, preacher, and leader.

Santos Elizondo

The life of Maye McReynolds cannot be fully told without relaying the story of her sister in ministry, Santos Elizondo. Maye led Santos, a 38-year-old native of Mexico, to faith while living in California. Soon after her conversion in 1905, Santos felt called to the ministry, despite the angry protestations and persecutions of her invalid husband.

Through the voice of an interpreter, Santos recalled her call to the ministry at the Seventh General Assembly:

> In 1905 the Lord saved me while I was ill in the county hospital in Los Angeles, California. The Lord turned my face back toward El Paso, Texas. For three months I wandered around among the Mexican churches of El Paso looking for that spiritual blessing in which I had found in the Church of the Nazarene in Los Angeles, California until one night I dreamed that a voice was saying to me, "If you want to feel what you felt in Los Angeles, you will have to start a church in El Paso, Texas." And the thought of me, a Mexican woman, starting a church—impossible—but when I looked to the Lord I saw all things were possible to them that love the Lord. The night that the Lord opened work in El Paso the Lord looked upon me and I had to obey Him. I hunted for the darkest corner and there was the people. I shut my eyes and began to pray. In that month I began to

work. I worked among my family, among my friends and neighbors, and in a short time I had gathered together a band of 25 people. I told Sister McReynolds and we organized a church. I was greatly persecuted, not by sinners, but by other pastors, but God blessed my soul and my people.[21]

Two years after Santos began evangelistic work in El Paso, S. D. Athans and his wife were sent to the El Paso church. Santos moved to Juarez, Mexico, a town separated from El Paso only by the Rio Grande. A church was organized in Juarez on March 7, 1907.

Maye McReynolds tells of how the mission in Juarez gained the approval of the Mexican government:

I remember with joy being in El Paso with our Sister [S]antos three years ago when [General] Madero and his troops were encamped across the border waiting to attack Juarez. Multitudes were crossing to visit the soldiers and officers so [S]antos and I decided to go over perchance we might preach the Gospel to the soldiers[.] We took with us about a thousand tracts[.] [A]lmost immediately after crossing the improvised suspension bridge which swayed under its human load and threatened to precipitate all in the waters below, the way opened to give out the portions and Gospels which proved an opportunity to "Preach Jesus" as they gathered together to receive the tracts, and we saw the tears flow from the stolid faces as we lifted up Jesus th[e] Savior of the world. We had the pleasure of speaking personally with Gen. Madero and the other officers . . . The battle of Juarez came on . . . 47 wounded soldiers [were] taken to El Paso hospital from Juarez to be cared for and ministered to by Santos and her faithful helpers in an improvised hospital . . . We soon opened a Mission in Juarez as Santos had almost immediately gained permission of Madero to preach in the publi[c] Plaza . . . Our Pen't Ch. of the Nazarene has the honor of having the first ordained Mexican woman preacher and also that of being the first to gain permission to hold public services the which is great gain for us.[22]

Santos' name officially appears as a deaconess in the

minutes of the 1910 Southern California District Assembly. By her own recollection she was ordained as an elder in 1911 in San Diego, and the 1912 district minutes acknowledge her as an elder in charge ministering in El Paso. Santos was formally appointed as a missionary to Juarez in 1916 and a letter dated September 15, 1925, in the foreign missions files contains her request for a new certificate signifying her official missionary status. Her original certificate had become torn and tattered due to continual showing at repeated border crossings.

Maye McReynolds describes Santos' work in a letter to the General Missionary Board convened at Chicago on October 5, 1910:

> We have good reports from Santos Elizondo at El Paso, Texas where this Mexican woman alone has by the power of God maintained the work of salvation at that place the past two and more years. She reports over 200 seekers at those altars the last year. 38 of th[e]se last month. [F]or over a year and a half no[t] one of our workers have [sic] been able to go to the assis[t]ance of this lone worker. It is felt by us that she is not able alone to bring into our church the proper results of her labor. The[re is] great opposition to our doctrines of holiness by five or more other established missions in that city, The feeling encouraged by many against a woman leader . . .[23]

The opposition to Santos' leadership was not solely over doctrine. Even one of her closest colleagues, S. D. Athans, resisted her in the role of church planter and pastor. In a letter dated October 5, 1915, Athans makes his opinions known:

> It seems to me that Bro. Gay and Sister McReynolds of Los Angeles, are and have been trying for some time, to put the Mexican work here and in Juarez, and especially Sister Santos Elizondo under their thumb. There has been a sort of correspondence, I believe, between them and Santos for some time, and judging from the attitude of Sister Santos

toward me and the work in El Paso, they are influencing her against me to the detriment of our work. Gay feels that I do not place Sister Santos high enough before the people and I ought to recognize the fact that she is an ordained minister in our church and as such she ought to be in the fore front but poor Bro. Gay and also Mrs. McReynolds don't seem to know the nature of the Mexican people well. I have told Gay that my experience in the work among the Mexican people has convinced me that, they *will not* have a woman as a *pastor* over them, they resent having a woman assume authority over them. The men in our Mexican churches especially are those who oppose woman's ministry as pastor, and I have not yet met a woman in the Mexican work anywhere who has any marked success to speak of in that capacity, but I believe in the ministry of women in the Gospel, and my honest conviction is that the best any woman missionary can do among the Mexican people is personal work, especially among those of their own sex, they can do successful deaconess work, teach in the Sunday School and exhort, teach in day schools, if they have the ability, but as pastors, my dear brother, in this work, a woman can do more to retard the work than to advance it. My impression is that Gay is hoping that if Mrs. McReynolds and Santos could work here together they could turn the world upside down . . . I believe I have worked harmoniously with Sister Santos and she is a good woman, teachable and humble, and I think I have tried to put her as high as common sense allows me to.[24]

During the course of her ministry, Santos' life would prove that Athan's claim that women were best fit for "personal work" among the Mexicans rather than serving in pastoral authority was narrow-minded. Santos showed, through her commitment to the Mexican people, that a woman can be effective in personal acts of mercy and teaching as well as pastoral leadership.

Listen to what another male colleague had to say about the church in Juarez after firsthand visits:

I was over in Juarez last night and at the end of the service some six came to the altar and I think about that number were baptized. Sister Santos is surely worthy and has suffered many things of the devil. *She is getting things done.* Any one who is not prejudiced will never speak evil of the work of women after seeing what she has done *and is doing.* She is not faultless nor are any of us but for *real performance* she is way ahead of many of us.[25]

Six years later, Rev. E. Y. Davis writes of another visit: "Sister Santos is a wonder. She just goes ahead and does things while we wonder how she does it. Her church is alive. Their missionary society had fourteen catholic women present last night. That is they *were* catholics. She starts them off this way and afterwards wins them to the gospel."[26]

Santos nearly single-handedly oversaw the work in Juarez for a span of nearly 35 years. During much of this time she ran the church, a day school, a women's society, an orphanage, and a medical clinic where she served as the midwife. During one year Santos gave medical attention to 118 maternity cases, attended 20 births, treated 114 for other diseases, and dispensed medicine to 203 others.

Funds and supplies were always low, and the inflation rate neared 100% many years in a row. Santos financed much of the mission work out of her own meager salary ($25.00 monthly in 1911) while caring for her husband and four adopted children. Often she expanded her household to feed and shelter many more.

The orphanage in Juarez opened in 1922. Seven orphans were left in El Paso and soon three more were sent from Colorado. Santos felt compelled to make provision for them despite scarce resources. By 1928 there were 43 orphans, and as the work grew, so did the resistance from the government. The Mexican government repeatedly tried to close the orphanage but each time they did, it was pointed out that the government had no other provisions for the children. Finally the president intervened between local officials and Santos to settle the matter. "We have investigated the work; there is no place for [the children] to go; and we have investigated the law, and we find that the law says, 'That no man shall have an orphanage in connection with the church,' but you are a woman so go to it."[27]

Rev. J. D. Scott, superintendent of the Mexican District, tells this heartwarming story in the *Quadrennial Report to the Sixth General Assembly* in 1923:

> Recently on a cool morning, about four o'clock, Sister Santos got up to cover some of the children, and said she realized keenly how near the winter was and no cover for the children. For a minute there was fear, and then she said, "Lord, you have those blankets somewhere for me. Make the one who has them bring them in." About nine o'clock that morning some one knocked on the door, and when she opened it there stood the president of the Catholic societies in Juarez, a beautiful cultured woman, saying, "Sister Santos, I woke up this morning thinking about you and your children and wondering what I could do to help you, and I thought of these blankets I had and was sure you could use them. Here are a dozen." Sister Santos said, "So you are the one who had my blankets . . ."[28]

A newspaper clipping in the Foreign Missions society correspondence file for 1926-28, recounts a similar story.

> Caring for 45 children and 10 destitute old folks seemed a task beyond a lone woman's strength and missionary's pay. Yet the matron could turn no one away . . . visitors at the home found 15 little girls huddled in a single bed! They were circled about the mattress, feet toward the center and covered by a bit of a blanket. Sister churches including Trinity Methodist bought 15 mattresses for the orphanage when the need was discovered.[29]

Santos certainly offered tangible aid to many she met,

but she also understood the need to find ways to support the individual's dignity as well. In a letter to E. G. Anderson, treasurer of the Foreign Missions society, Rev. Elizondo describes the Christmas offering of 1924. She distributed half of her own saved offering among the children to be put into the collection plate. One of the girls later responded, "I dreamed that I was big and some of the money collected yesterday was sen[t] to me because I was a missionary [to] Mexico." Another of the girls said to the others, "Don't it feel nice when you give something to help."[30]

The ever-compassionate Sister Elizondo is also recognized by another undated news story from an El Paso newspaper, also found in the Foreign Missions society files, as the one who ministered to Agapito Rueda, the convicted murderer of a payroll guard who was slain during the "G. H. & S. A. holdup expedition." The prison social worker tells of Rueda's agitation and terror of the electric chair. She convinced him to come to the prison chapel where "Sister Santos explained the spiritual rebirth. He got on his knees and prayed, with tears streaming down his face he told the Lord he had always sinned. Suddenly he got up smiling." After this experience, Rueda attended chapel regularly, read the Bible constantly, and testified to his conversion. When he was executed, he asked the guard to, "'Turn the juice on just a little at first.' The warden complied. Rueda flinched, then gazed upward and murmured: 'Lord, receive my spirit.'" The man's body lay in state at the Juarez Church of the Nazarene before burial.

Santos characteristically was drawn to the disenfranchised. Perhaps this was because her own life was one of hardship. Her zealous proclamation of the gospel raised the ire of local priests and set her in opposition to the predominantly Catholic society. At one point Santos was required to cease her work as a nurse and midwife. The newly appointed doctor in charge of the health department was a strict Catholic and did not want a Protestant woman offering medical assistance to the poor. In 1931 Santos received threats from a terrorist group that called themselves "the scarlet viper." The group threatened to rob Santos, harm the orphans, and burn the church building. Santos' response in this situation is evidence of her strong faith. She wrote to the Department of Foreign Missions declaring, "I testify that even with these threats, I feel the perfect peace of the Lord in my heart, and am afraid of nothing."[31]

By 1935 the changing tenor of the Mexican government again put restrictions on the church at Juarez, but by this time Santos and her flock were wise to the ways of the state. Superintendent David said this of the church in his annual report:

> The Juarez church is in the best condition I have ever seen it. The religious laws and recent restrictions of the government have only served to make our people more faithful and determined. Many new people attend the services, even Catholics are coming. And thank God for Sister Santos Elizondo and her faithful workers. The Lord has prepared them for such a time like this. They are wise enough not to infringe upon the laws and spiritual enough to feed the people the bread of life. Our church at Juarez is a spiritual clearing house doing business for the Lord and taking care of the needs of the people systematically and thoroughly. I do not know of any church so well organized and actively functioning in every way as this one. And it has all come about thru prayer. Sister Santos is certainly a woman of God and mighty in prayer.[32]

The little we know of Santos' personal spirituality beyond her enormous capacity for loving action is shown in her visionary experiences. In a handwritten, undated letter, she recounts one such experience.

> In the months of February, March and April I had many maternity cases and the heavy work with loss of sleep

made me seriously ill. I saw myself in the valley of the shadow of death, but the 23rd Psalm was fulfilled in me. . . . One night I felt myself dying and cried to my God with all faith. I slept for a moment and I saw a being who said to me, "Fear not, you are not going to die. You still have a work to do for your God. If He was ready to take you He would have revealed it to you; you are going to live a little longer." I awoke full of confidence in that vision and told it to the dear sisters who were gathered around me.

Until the time of her death Santos remained actively in charge of the Juarez mission work. Guadalupe Elizondo Navarro, Mrs. Santos' daughter, sent a chronicle of her mother's last hours to the Nazarene officials the day after Santos died on March 3, 1941. Mrs. Navarro remembered that on the morning of Saturday, March 1, Santos was sad, heavyhearted, and suffering greatly. She kept asking God why the person she asked for had not been sent. When asked by her daughter who she wanted to see or talk to Santos replied without really answering, "If I am worthy, I want my Father to send him to me if it is His sweet will."

By afternoon a knock came on the door, and the pastor of the El Paso Church of the Nazarene stood outside. When Santos heard who it was, she prayed a prayer of thanksgiving, then instructed her daughter, "No, don't open the door until you make sure it is Brother Hocker, if it is anybody else don't let them in . . ." Brother Hocker entered and Santos' face lit up. They talked a bit and Santos requested the Lord's Supper.

Mrs. Navarro gives a moving account of Santos' response to this answered prayer:

After a little while they [Rev. Hocker and other friends that later joined him] left, but from that moment on she was a different person, and her spirit seemed [calm] . . . she kept saying, "Thank you, thank you my loving Father, because you granted what I had been asking . . . once more you have shown me that I am still your child and that you have not abandoned me. Now I ask dear Lord, that you take me and let me rest; I have suffered much, but this has been a great day for me; . . . Now I only ask that you fill [my daughter and granddaughter] with your spirit and help them with your great power, that they may continue faithful to Christ and may have mercy and love for my dear little orphans and may care for them with your help and guidance.[33]

Santos' moving prayer prompted her daughter to accept the mantle of ministry that her mother had so faithfully carried for many decades.

Thousands of friends and community leaders walked the aisle of Santos' small church in Juarez to pay their last respects. Her obituary records that the mourners "came from all walks of life, Catholics as well as protestants. Even the leaders of the Catholic Church came to pay their respects and they remained for the service."[34] Drawing people of all creeds and personal circumstances to her, both in life and death, Santos was truly a great woman of God.

Elsie Wallace

In 1897, Elsie Marble Wallace, a Nebraska native, moved to Spokane, Wash., with her husband, DeLance Wallace. This couple had experienced sanctification as a result of revival meetings four years earlier while living in Kansas. The Wallaces brought a holiness zeal with them to the Northwest and organized the Washington Holiness Association shortly after they arrived.

The flourishing of the Church of the Nazarene in southern California did not go without notice in the rest of the Northwest. In 1902 Phineas Bresee accepted an invitation to travel to Spokane, Wash., at the behest of DeLance and Elsie Wallace. The Wallaces led, with William Lee, the John 3:16 rescue mission in "a block almost literally filled on its four sides with saloons and places of wickedness."[35]

C. W. Ruth, who served as assistant general superintendent to Bresee in the new denomination, conducted a revival in the Spokane mission in January 1902. By the end of the week he had organized the mission into the first Nazarene church outside California. Elsie Wallace had superintended the mission since 1899 and was selected by unanimous vote as pastor over the 50 charter members, the decision subject to Bresee's approval.[36]

Elsie took charge immediately, and wrote a letter the very next day that was published in the *Nazarene Messenger:*

> We wish four dozen manuals, also any thing else you think a new church needs. Now Doctor [Bresee], we are loathe to *increase* the cumbersome duties upon your shoulders but we are just *"new beginners"* and need fatherly advice and prayer, and won't you get us under your care, that we may be at our *very best for God.* I feel my utter helplessness and ignorance and our Lord must give wisdom, for this work is His, and we His Bride. Hallelujah! At your earliest convenience—we hope not later than in April—we want you to come up and "straighten us out," and in every way shepherd your "youngest lambs."[37]

When Bresee arrived later in July, Elsie's power and competence as a leader was confirmed during an ordination service held in her own home. Elsie Wallace became in actuality the first woman ordained in the Church of the Nazarene because she did not first receive a preacher's license, as did Lucy Knott who was ordained some six months later.

During its first six months of affiliation with the Nazarenes, the Spokane church grew to more than 80 members "made up largely of clear-headed and anointed workers."[38]

When it came time for Elsie to give her report at the First Annual Assembly of the Northwest District in July of

1905, she gladly declared, "The Lord is giving the greatest victory in the history of the Church and bringing men and women to the altar at almost every service. The church now numbers more than 200 members. The condition of the work is splendid."[39] This growth in membership occurred even though the church was forced to relocate to a tent when the previous location was "rented away from the young church." When the tent was destroyed in a windstorm, the church moved to a blacksmith shop where they worshiped until 1907 when they were able to purchase a lot and erect a tabernacle.[40]

After leading the Spokane church to solid ground, the Wallaces and other workers spearheaded the organization of Nazarene churches in Garfield, Wash.; Ashland, Oreg.; Boise, Idaho; and later in Walla Walla and Seattle, Wash.

In 1907 Elsie accepted the call to the small and struggling Seattle First Church at the urging of Dr. Bresee. Three years later, when DeLance became the district superintendent, Elsie began revival work. A tent meeting in Walla Walla resulted in the organization of a new church that prevailed upon Elsie to stay and become their pastor, a position she held for nine years.

An article in *The Pentecostal Messenger* reports on a revival at the Walla Walla church: "The Nazarene church here is one of the best we have seen in numbers and unity. The pastor, Mrs. DeLance Wallace, is indeed one of the best pastors we had ever seen anywhere, and is doing a great work."[41]

While the Wallaces lived in Walla Walla, their son, Lew, became ill and his father recalled a few months later, "His life hung by a very slender thread for 10 weeks. Mrs. Wallace has not yet fully recovered from the nervous strain, but the Lord graciously spared Lew's life despite the physicians assurance that he could not recover."[42]

By 1919 the Walla Walla church was the largest on the

district, claiming a membership of 210 with 381 enrolled in Sunday School. The district minutes describe the church as "deeply spiritual and very aggressive."[43]

Early in 1920 the current district superintendent, Rev. C. Warren Jones, received appointment as a missionary to Japan. Elsie Wallace was appointed to serve as district superintendent for the last four months of the assembly year by John W. Goodwin, general superintendent.

A letter from the general superintendent to the president of C.W.R. & N. Co., the regional railroad, provides a glimpse into the scope of her responsibilities:

> Elsie M. Wallace of Walla Walla, Washington has been appointed as District Superintendent of our Northwestern District . . . We would thank you to furnish her transportation over your lines West of The Dalles and North of Pendleton Oregon in lieu of that furnished to the Rev. Jones.[44]

Elsie Wallace apparently fulfilled her role as district superintendent well because the district minutes from 1920 contain a resolution that expresses thanks to Dr. Goodwin "for his wise choice of Sister Elsie M. Wallace to act as District Superintendent." A later resolution expresses the deep sadness felt by those on the district as the Wallaces, referred to as "the father and mother of our great Northwest District," prepared to move to Kansas City, where DeLance Wallace had accepted the position as the general manager of the denominational publishing house. The minutes poignantly state that the Wallaces "seem to be part of us, and we refuse to give them up. Their lives will continue to pulsate in the life of the District, and down through the years, if God does not restore them to us, we know that their influence will go on and on, inspiring, cheering, and helping."[45]

Mrs. Wallace did return to the Northwest and served as pastor of the church in Seattle a second time. She then served as district evangelist for eight years and traveled throughout the Northwest and Canada.

The life of an itinerant evangelist proved to be a demanding, lonely task, as can be felt in this letter Elsie sent to a friend she addresses as Sister Hawkins:

> This is Sunday, but I am going to drop you a note. I am so lonesome. Reached here about 6 P.M. last evening—they met me at Corvalis and we drove 30 miles over the Alsen Mt. I was so frightened, honestly Sr. Hawkins, I felt I would give $50.00 to be home. It had rained and the road was *so* slippery. I think it was more because of knowing of Bro. Barnett's car skidding. Well I am here at the Parsonage. Have a room upstairs. Have a stove just outside my door in a room I can use too, a nice clean comfortable bed, so I am very comfortable. I thank the Lord for all this. I wish you were with me. I just wondered how I could stand it for 2 weeks, but I *will* and will be glad I did . . . Our meeting started very well this morning, not a large crowd at all, but quite a few. I asked Bro. Reeder (the pastor) how many were there. He said in the town and surrounding community there was about 200. So you see I haven't much to draw on, *but* they need the Gospel here as all places.
>
> Say do you know that croup was more than I thought[?] I am really not over it yet. I have to be so careful all the time. It seems to take the breath right out of me. Guess I'll soon be o.k. again, however. I wish you would take a few minutes and write me *here.* When I got here there was a letter for me from Vi. I was so glad. It helped a lot I can tell you. If I am home I hope we can go the next all day meeting together.[46]

Elsie later moved to California where she held pastorates in Ontario, La Habra, and Wilmington. When she retired from the active ministry in 1941, Elsie Wallace had given more than four decades of her life to the cause of holiness and the Church of the Nazarene. She died in Pasadena, Calif., on February 22, 1946, at the age of 77.[47] Fittingly, Elsie's pastor, another early woman minister in the denomination, Rev. Mrs. Emma French, presided at her funeral.

Elsie Wallace is to be remembered as a true pastor. In a

report to the Seattle church in 1928, she read a poem that shows she had a pastor's heart:[48]

> *I love Thy Church, O God!*
> *Her walls before Thee stand,*
> *Dear as the apple of Thine eye,*
> *And graven on Thy hand.*

> *For her my tears shall fall;*
> *For her my pray'rs ascend;*
> *To her my cares and toils be giv'n*
> *Till toils and cares shall end.*

Elsie and DeLance worked side by side in ministry from the time of their marriage in 1890; she as the active elder, he as an ordained minister who chose to remain in secular employment during much of his life. DeLance recognized that Elsie possessed better gifts and graces for pastoral ministry; so he used his financial and personal support to allow Elsie to pursue her calling. During the years he served as district superintendent of the Northwest District, he was able to continue with his support while he built the district infrastructure. The Wallaces had two children, one that died in infancy and their son, Lew, who preceded Elsie in death by four years.

The common link that holds these varied women's lives together is more than geographical. Each of these ministers of the gospel saw a need, stepped in, and filled it.

Lucy Knott worked with young girls and then preached at the Mateo Street mission, where she ministered to the people before they were a congregation. Her ministry presence among them led to her election as pastor and subsequent ordination.

Maye McReynold's heart was moved by the plight of the Mexican immigrants she encountered through her work with the railroads. Her compassion led to action that her church then sponsored, yet the impetus for caring began with her.

Santos Elizondo wanted to share her newfound faith with the people of her country of birth. Without funding or recognition, but with the support of Maye McReynolds, she labored to build a church and organize outreach efforts to help soothe the effects of poverty in her native Mexico. She started a congregation, which her denomination then claimed. She cared for orphans who landed on her doorstep, later organizing an orphanage that became a part of the Nazarene mission work. Time and time again she took the initiative, and sponsorship followed.

Elsie Wallace, like Lucy Knott, exercised pastoral ministry for a group before they were a formal congregation. The fruit of her presence among them was evident in their choice of her as their pastor. Her successful ministry then led to calls from other churches.

Ordination for the women of the Western Church of the Nazarene was the second step of ministry. Each of these women responded, as divinely called ministers, to people in need. The church recognized and supported their gifts and graces by conferring ordination. These women acted on an inner compulsion to minister and out of a conviction that God, indeed, needed them as leaders in order to spread the good news to a needy world.

3

Women Preachers in the Northeast

While the Church of the Nazarene established itself in southern California, individual churches that would later unite with the denomination were already organized and taking in members in the Northeast. The development of holiness churches in New England preceded those in southern California by over a decade.

Boston was a locale of major influence as the holiness movement developed. The *Guide to Holiness*, a periodical that was long a catalyst for the movement, was founded there in 1839, and Boston University taught the doctrine during the final decades of the 19th century. New England provided an environment hospitable to the involvement of women in the holiness movement. The evangelistic efforts of holiness revivalist Lizzie Boyd eventually led to the formation of the People's Evangelical Church in Providence, R.I. This church would be the oldest congregation brought into the union with the California Nazarenes. Work among the poor of Washington, D.C., was begun by two sisters, Phoebe and Sarah Hall, members of the Society of Friends. And of course, the influence of Antoinette Brown Blackwell and Phoebe Palmer in separate areas of New York state cannot be forgotten.

Three women who early and long served the Church of the Nazarene, Susan Norris Fitkin, Martha Curry, and

Olive Winchester will be highlighted later in this chapter after a short history of how the denomination originated in the Northeast.

Nazarene Origins in the Northeast

During the late 1880s H. F. Reynolds, an energetic young Methodist minister from Vermont, along with his brother E. E. Reynolds, and a lay couple, O. J. Copeland and his wife, organized the Vermont Holiness Association to promote holiness revivals throughout the state. All of the association's activities were to be conducted in complete loyalty to the Methodist church. The work went well, and by 1892 H. F. Reynolds requested a leave of absence from his ministerial appointment so that he could give all his time to organizing and leading revivals throughout Vermont. As Reynolds moved from town to town, he met other holiness advocates along the Northeastern seaboard.

In the following years, O. J. Copeland moved to Brooklyn to open a granite business where he became involved with the loose association of holiness churches fostered by William H. Hoople. By October 1895 Reynolds also moved to Brooklyn and joined Hoople's association. Because he possessed a strong bent toward organization, Reynolds was able to incorporate the Association of Pentecostal Churches in America less than a year after he moved to New York.

He is described as "the most able and aggressive home missionary evangelist as well as the most effective fund raiser,"[1] and therefore soon became prominent in Hoople's association. In time, he even took on the singular challenge of overseeing the foreign mission work that the association had already begun in India and the Cape Verde Islands.

It wasn't long before visitors from New England to

California and back began to notice the similarities between the work of Hoople's association and the newly organized Church of the Nazarene, and by January 1906 the missionary committee of the Association of Pentecostal Churches invited Dr. Bresee to come to their annual meeting. Bresee was unable to attend but sent a representative. Visits back and forth commenced, and the union between the Association of Pentecostal Churches and the Church of the Nazarene was formalized as a contingent of Nazarenes, led by Dr. Bresee, traveled East to attend the 1907 annual meeting of the association. The two groups concluded that the contents of the *Manual of the Church of the Nazarene* aptly covered the essential points of importance to both groups. There was only one major sticking point on the issue of congregational rule over property and pastoral arrangements, which resulted in a compromise. New England congregations organized before the union could continue to hold property in their own names, but those organized later would belong to the denomination. And the system of having churches call their own pastors was acceptable to all of the congregations. Many also preferred limiting the role of the general superintendent to one of approving a local congregation's choice rather than giving the general superintendent the right to appoint new ministers at will.

With these basic agreements in place, member churches of the Association of Pentecostal Churches were encouraged to submit suggestions for a Manual revision to the First General Assembly of the Church of the Nazarene to be held in Chicago in 1907. At that assembly, a united General Missionary Board was formed to oversee both foreign and home mission efforts. H. F. Reynolds was elected to the dual role of executive secretary of the General Missionary Board and general superintendent. Thus Bresee from the West and Reynolds from the East shouldered the responsibility of moving the new denomination forward under the name Pentecostal Church of the Nazarene.

Susan Norris Fitkin

In 1896 one of the 15 churches in the Northeast that joined with the Association of Pentecostal Churches came into existence through the efforts of Susan Norris, a Canadian evangelist who was serving as a pastor in Vermont.

Susan Norris was born on March 31, 1870, in Ely, Que. At the age of 17 she experienced severe health problems, and doctors diagnosed her with cancer and gave her a year or two to live. About this time, a traveling Quaker preacher conducted special meetings near Susan's home. This series of meetings prompted Susan to become a regular attender of the Quaker meeting. Soon after, while reading her Bible Susan experienced conversion.

Later in the same year Susan was stricken with typhoid fever and almost died. While those surrounding her thought she was dying, Susan recalls a vivid vision of a dark valley with a brightly illumined gate at the end. She felt God's clear presence, and when she was asked if she wanted to cross into heaven she replied, "Whatever is Thy will; I would not turn my hand over to decide!" She then slept and awoke knowing she would get well.

Within several months Susan was well enough to travel to visit her brothers, and while away from home she experienced a call to preach one December night. She dreamed of the Second Coming. Jesus appeared as she was in a small chapel with friends and family. Filled with excitement she ran toward the door to meet Him but was taken aback by the sound of wailing behind her. Most of those in the chapel were anguished and afraid of the presence of Christ. Then Susan heard an audible voice declare, "Go you into all the world, and preach the gospel to every creature."

Susan's own words describe the power of her sense of calling:

> I was astonished, for I was still an invalid, with no hope of living more than two or three years, but the memory of my dream, and all those people begging for mercy when it was *too late* had so stirred my heart that I at once replied, "Oh, Lord, I will go, but you know how frail I am; you will have to take all the responsibility." He assured me that He would, and a great peace filled my soul.
>
> This was such a clear, definite call that I never doubted it, and as the months went by I often wondered when and how God would open the door, and where my work was to be. I thought it must be to a foreign field.[2]

Due to her unpredictable health, Susan found no open avenue to fulfill her calling in a foreign land. She involved herself in the work of local young people's groups, but she felt concerned about obeying her calling and asked God for clarification as to how she was to serve. She recalls, "Suddenly my eyes were riveted on these words which I did not know were in the Book—'I have not called thee to a people of a strange tongue and of a hard language.'"[3] Despite her initial disappointment at not being called to minister overseas, Susan accepted this new direction and felt at peace.

In the summer of 1892 Susan was sent by the local Society of Friends to a convention in New York City. At the meetings there she met Rev. J. W. Malone and his wife, who were just opening a Missionary and Bible Training Institute in Cleveland, Ohio. Susan was determined to attend in the fall. The institute provided study and practical opportunities for mission work through "The Whosoever Will Mission." After she enrolled, the institute gave her a Sunday afternoon assignment that involved teaching a band of street boys who had taunted every previous teacher into resignation. Susan patiently worked with the group, ranging in age from 12 to 16, and, after first winning their friendship, saw many of their lives transformed.

During that first winter at Bible school, Susan was chosen to accompany a woman evangelist to Indiana where special evangelistic meetings were scheduled. The meetings were so successful that Susan stayed on while the evangelist moved to the next appointment. The meetings continued, but with little preaching until on Sunday morning Susan felt the Lord had given her a message during her quiet time even though she had no intention of publicly proclaiming any sermon. After a hymn was sung and one of the elders prayed, one of the women elders "leaned over to me and said, 'Feel perfectly free, dear, thee go ahead and give the message the Lord has given thee,'" and Susan did. Thus Susan offered her first sermon, and many gathered around her afterward to tell her of the blessings they had received. Susan writes of that day, "It was all so wonderful, and I was thankful and happy in the assurance that the Lord had indeed chosen me to preach the glorious gospel, even though I was not to be a personal messenger to foreign lands."[4]

Susan then returned to complete her studies and afterward took a summer placement as an assistant pastor in northern Michigan, but in the fall a family illness summoned her home. Soon, however, Susan received a request to assist in evangelistic meetings in Vermont, which she accepted, and the church was so blessed by her ministry that they asked her to stay on as their pastor. Sometime before this, Susan had already been made a minister by the Friends Society, so she willingly accepted the pastorate of the Vermont church. After only one year, however, Susan moved to another pastorate in the Green Mountains of Vermont. Toward the end of her first year there the chairman of the Evangelistic Committee of the New York District of the Friends Society visited Susan's church and persuaded the reluctant young pastor that her gifts were much needed in evangelistic work in his state. Again, Susan stepped out into unknown territory.

It was a step that would transform her spiritual life, for while Susan conducted her first revival in New York state, she attended a nearby holiness convention. As she listened to the very first message, she fell under great desire to have the second blessing, but pride and reluctance plagued her. Her own position as a preacher in the midst of a successful revival made her worry that people would think her backslidden if she obeyed the inner urging and prayed at the altar. She finally did go forward, however, and sought the experience of full salvation. Then she waited and felt nothing, but she testified to a cleansing from all sin as she was encouraged to do.

She left the meeting, and an inner battle began to rage. Doubts that she was no different than she had been that morning plagued her spirit. By the time her own evening revival service rolled around, Susan was so emotionally exhausted that she asked another evangelist to preach. On the way to the service, Susan resolved to believe that she was fully clean from sin even if she never *felt* anything that confirmed her belief. Holding fast to this decision brought back her composure and inner peace. Then, during the service, as her colleague began to preach Susan was unexpectedly overcome with the Holy Spirit: "Suddenly the chapel roof seemed to be cleft asunder; the heavens were rent; and shafts of heavenly light like sunbeams shot down directly into my heart, filling and thrilling my soul. I shouted and laughed, trying to control the avalanche so as not to disconcert the Preacher."[5]

Susan's efforts at self-control were to no avail. Others in the congregation began to shout and laugh in the blessing of the Spirit. The congregation was as astonished as Susan had been. She had always prided herself on "being a demure little Quaker maiden" who didn't appreciate exuberant displays during services. Now this unexpected outburst made her ask herself, "What did it all mean?" But she happily concluded that the Holy Spirit had come to fully abide in her life and in the lives of others in attendance. She then rose and took the pulpit to declare how the Spirit had been at work in her life that day. As a result, many others earnestly sought the blessing of holiness that night.

The success of that revival led to the scheduling of other meetings throughout the district. Susan was sent out with Abram E. Fitkin, whom she describes as "a very gifted young evangelist, who enjoyed the blessing of holiness and preached it very clearly and definitely."[6] An account of one of their joint revival meetings appears in the March 26, 1896, issue of the *Christian Witness and Advocate of Bible Holiness.*

> We have just closed a series of meetings which were conducted at Cornwall, N.Y., a town of some 5,000 inhabitants. The Lord himself was present in mighty convicting, converting and sanctifying power. The place had not known what a Holy Ghost revival was for 20 years, though various attempts had been made, but with little success. We had been cautioned before we commenced the meetings, not to preach holiness in the general meetings, but simply [to] speak and preach on the work of conversion. We did not feel thus led, but [on the] contrary, we were convinced of God that definite preaching and teaching on holiness was needed and through it, God gave victory over sin and Satan . . . and brought about 100 souls unto himself.[7]

For the next six months Susan and Abram traveled the state and found that they worked exceedingly well together; in fact, they soon found themselves in love. They married in the summer of 1896 and continued as co-evangelists for several years.

Susan recounts one specific revival in a railroad town. There was no evangelical church in the town or surrounding areas, so the Fitkins sought to rent a building for services. The only available building was a blacksmith shop with a year-long lease. Trusting in God's provision, they personally paid the first portion of the year's rent and purchased chairs and other amenities to hold the services. By the time they had paid to advertise the revival, they were sorely short of funds and decided they must stay in the blacksmith shop and sleep on the chairs. A knock on the door brought another sort of provision. A couple identifying themselves as "friends" had watched the Fitkins' activities and felt compelled to invite the young couple to stay at their house for the duration of the meetings. Within weeks, 60 new converts were organized into a church. Great was the rejoicing over the work of God, yet Susan and Abram faced a new dilemma. What were they to do with such a boisterous, vibrant, evangelistic church? The surrounding Quaker churches were quiet and conservative and not open to demonstrative worship.

Abram felt the new church should join with the Association of Holiness Churches (one of the groups that later joined the Association of Pentecostal Churches of America). Susan was reluctant because she had been a member of the Society of Friends for years and did not wish to change church affiliation. She prayed and wept for days before accepting this move as God's will. Eventually, however, both the church and the pastors, Susan and Abram, decided to join ranks with the "little band of despised, struggling, but victorious Holiness people."[8]

By 1900 the Fitkins were full members of the Association of Pentecostal Churches of America. During the annual assembly of the churches, a women's missionary society was announced, and Susan Fitkin became a charter member. The next year she became president, and her lifelong interest in foreign missions became the continuing focus for years to come.

When the Association of Pentecostal Churches merged with the Church of the Nazarene in 1907, Susan was officially ordained as an elder in the new denomination. Dr. Bresee presided and Susan recounts the service: "[It was a] memorable occasion but was only the human sanction to God's work. For years before he had definitely spoken these precious words to my heart, 'Ye have not chosen me, but I have chosen you, and ordained you, that ye should go and bring forth fruit,' and had He not verified it again and again?"[9]

Susan's experience is one that is seen in many of the first generation of ordained women elders. Ordination was granted by the church as a public testimony and confirmation of God's calling. Susan knew that the real authority for her to serve the church and preach publicly did not depend on the church's recognition as much as on her own deeply rooted sense of divine appointment.

Susan and Abram soon added family responsibilities to their ministry. Abram began a new career as a Wall Street financier, and Susan continued to preach on Sundays as opportunity allowed and to serve the fledgling women's missionary society while her children were small.

It was while Susan lived on Long Island that a local Methodist minister was called to his ailing father's bedside. During this absence, Susan and Abram filled in at the church. The minister had told the Fitkins that his church needed revival, yet he feared losing many members if he preached holiness messages. He encouraged his Nazarene friends to preach whatever messages were given to them by the Lord. The Fitkins obliged, but during this time, Abram was summoned away on an extended business trip, so Susan took over the church responsibilities. During the five week period, she gave regular altar calls, and many seekers responded so that upon his return, the minister was amazed and delighted at what God had done during his absence.

A few years later, in 1914 when the Fitkins' oldest son, Raleigh, was 10 years old, he was stricken with an ailment that resembled appendicitis. The doctors felt the first series of attacks were not worrisome. Yet when a more severe attack occurred with unrelenting pain, an operation was advised but scheduled a few weeks hence. Raleigh did not survive the operation.

Susan was greatly grieved and longed for her dear son, but comfort came through two divine encounters. The first occurred while Susan prayed a few days before Raleigh's death. She felt God told her that Raleigh was to be taken, "that it was for the best, and while I bowed in submission to His will, for days and weeks after he had gone, my heart longed for my beautiful boy, my first-born, who had always seemed almost like an angel sent down to us from the skies."[10]

The second divine word came to Susan in a night vision, and it was this experience that she attests brought her real lasting comfort. In her dream Susan saw Raleigh, all tanned and healthy, standing at the foot of her bed dressed in a bathing suit. His face glowed with happiness. As Susan reached out for him she awoke and great sorrow overtook her as she realized he was not physically there. Then she heard the Lord gently say, "He is with me, and so happy; you must learn to rejoice in his joy." Inner peace filled Susan's heart and from that day forward she was able to envision Raleigh in heaven, "happy and blest, safely sheltered, and waiting to welcome me Home."[11]

In 1915, during the third General Assembly of the Church of the Nazarene held in Kansas City, women's involvement in missionary work was formally recognized. A national organization, the Women's Foreign Missionary Society (WFMS), was approved, and Susan's official tenure as president, a role she filled until 1948, began.

Susan made her first of several journeys abroad in 1926, at her own expense. She visited the British Isles District where she found many women involved in the work of the WFMS. By 1928, just 13 years after its formation, the missionary organization claimed 17,000 members and had raised $237,000 for missionary endeavors.

The society then began to prepare missionary study books and to organize the youth. The juniors, children in grades four to six, supported orphans and missionary children. The Prayer and Fasting League encouraged weekly prayer meetings for missions. By 1932, during the depression, 1,150 societies had been organized with 25,000 members on the rolls, and the financial giving topped $450,000. The WFMS was making a definite mark on the denomination.

During this period of unparalleled growth, Susan undertook a special project. A new hospital was needed in Swaziland, Africa, and the WFMS rose to the challenge of raising the money. In the summer of 1927, 13 years after Raleigh's death, Susan Fitkin and Mrs. Paul Bresee, Phineas' daughter-in-law, traveled by boat for four weeks to reach Cape Town, South Africa. An express train conducted them the remaining 1,500 miles to Swaziland, where they were met by Harmon F. Schmelzenbach, legendary Nazarene missionary to Africa. The group switched their luggage into Schmelzenbach's car and drove through the moonlight until midnight to reach the hospital station.

Susan had come these thousands of miles to be present at the dedication of the new Raleigh Fitkin Memorial Hospital. She spoke at the dedication service and especially mentioned the role Nazarene women had played in helping make the hospital possible.

A native service followed in which expressions of gratitude were made by several preachers and a representative of the Swazi King. Susan's words about her departed son especially touched the Swazi nationals, many of whom had walked up to 85 miles to be present at the celebration. Susan records the tender response of the national leaders:

They mentioned very tenderly the mother *whose little boy had been interested in them,* and said this mother should not feel bad because he had gone to Heaven, for now she had many sons and daughters in Africa. They wanted to give her an African name, so they called her "U-no-ban-tu," which means "Mother of nations," but they wanted it to especially mean "Mother of the Bantu People."[12]

Susan and Mrs. Bresee went from the hospital dedication to a camp meeting held at the oldest Nazarene mission station in Swaziland, Schmelzenbach station. There the sunrise meetings, conducted by the national preachers, especially touched Susan. She had a keen eye for recognizing the contributions made to the church by women around the world and she recorded her impression of "the wife of Enoch the Evangelist, who was also a preacher."

"'I can't understand how anybody can be so full, but it is the Holy Spirit in my heart . . .' How her face shone; it was positively beautiful! She was dressed in white, with a black kerchief tied over her hair and looked like a veritable African saint. Through her, the blessing of the Lord fell upon the entire congregation."[13]

Susan's second missionary excursion took her to Mexico in 1928. She attended the District Assembly in Mexico City during the Fiesta de Guadalupe and eagerly learned about the religious beliefs of the Mexican people while trying to understand what meaning and inner peace they received through their offerings of expensive flowers and exotic dances. The poverty and anguish Susan saw on many faces grieved her tender missionary heart. Upon leaving Mexico City, Mrs. Fitkin circled through Juarez to visit Santos Elizondo. Mrs. Fitkin attests to having been in attendance at the first anniversary of the dedication of the Juarez church several years before. She describes the mission station, a "little white church" on the corner with Santos' house and orphanage flanking the other two sides of a square with a children's playground in the middle. The first WFMS in Mexico was organized and prospered in Juarez. Santos Elizondo and Susan Fitkin shared the missionary spirit and deeply appreciated each other.

The next trip abroad Susan undertook was to Barbados and Trinidad in 1929. She records her visits to several Hindu temples, and her walks among the destitute Indian people in Trinidad awaiting deportation due to food and employment shortages. The spiritual and economic conditions moved Susan to deep compassion. She visited Panama and Central America in 1935, Japan, China, and Korea the following year, and Argentina in 1937.

Another later trip to Hawaii, suggested by Susan's doctors after her lifelong frail physical condition worsened, allowed her to visit a Buddhist temple. The modern building resembled a Protestant church, and to Susan's surprise the priest was a woman, a white American woman. The service closely resembled that of a Christian service in format, and Susan recalled hearing that Buddhists of that day were adopting evangelistic methods similar to those of Christian missionaries. This experience moved Susan to commit herself to trust God for renewed health so that she could continue to follow her sense of calling to enable Christian missionary efforts through the world. A few months later Susan received a clean bill of health, and she continued to serve the denomination as president of the WFMS and as a member of the General Board, the highest legislative board of the denomination.

Upon her retirement from the missionary society, Susan was presented with a check for $70,000, designated to erect Bible training schools in Japan, China, British Honduras, and the Philippines. During the more than three decades that she led the efforts of Nazarene women for the purposes of missions, $6,000,000 was raised and 80,000 women were enrolled as members.

Susan Fitkin died at the age of 81 on October 18, 1951, while living in Oakland, Calif. The Memoirs Committee that convened at the 1956 General Assembly records that "Influencing people through countless letters, articles, and messages constituted an important part of her ministry. One cannot evaluate the results of her prayers, her compassion for the lost, and her untiring efforts to send the Gospel to the ends of the earth."[14]

Martha E. Curry

Susan Fitkin embodied both a missionary spirit and evangelistic enthusiasm. Martha E. Curry, a New England compatriot, exemplified the gifts of a pastoral calling and zeal for evangelism. Her heart was specifically attuned to the needs of the American church.

Martha Eva Curry entered this world on June 16, 1867, in Chelsea, Mass. By her own account, Martha grew up in a house that was "absolutely godless." She recalls, "I was a very worldly young woman, dancing, going to the theater, breaking the Sabbath, loving dress, and wanting nothing to do with religion."

When her family moved to Stoneham, Mass., an aunt invited Martha, who was nearing 16, to Sunday School where her Sunday School teacher and the leaders at the local YMCA took an interest in her. Some months later, Martha declined an invitation to attend a revival service in the Methodist church, but when the time came to go to the service, her teacher knocked at her door anyway. Martha reluctantly attended. That night Martha felt the evangelist was preaching right at her; she even wrongly suspected her teacher had told him all about her in advance! Martha vowed not to return for another meeting, but her teacher again returned to her house unbidden and took Martha to the service, ushering her up to the second row. Martha recalls that night vividly:

The evangelist not only preached at me, but God talked to me. Before the sermon was over I was having an argument with God. He led me over my life, and showed me the opportunities I had had in the last three months to seek Him, and the people who had prayed for me, and the conviction that had been put on my heart. And He also said to me, "Now, young woman, you must yield to Me." And when the invitation was given I went to the altar.

There at the altar I began confessing my sins. Nobody had told me what to do or say. I had been in only two revival services. But my conviction was so deep that I poured my heart to God in pleading for forgiveness. I prayed until I had nothing else to pray for. Then I didn't know what to do.

Presently the evangelist had [the congregation] sing, "Just As I Am Without One Plea . . ." Just as they reached the last line, the evangelist came and touched me on the shoulder, and [said] "Believe it."

I did believe! And my soul was filled with the glory of God. Oh, what a change! What a change! I knew that all my sins were forgiven. And not only that, I knew that I was saved, that I was born of God.[15]

Some six weeks later, Martha felt her old temper return, a feeling that she confessed at a class meeting. Then and there she was told there was a second work of grace. This new information only served to make Martha angrier! "Why didn't I get it all when I was converted?" she asked.

The same faithful Sunday School teacher loaned Martha a book on sanctification. The following Sunday as she read it God spoke to Martha, "Now, my child, you see your need. And you see that I can sanctify people wholly. Get right down on your knees here, ask me to do it, and I will."

Strong-willed Martha refused. She continued to attend church, and additionally began to lead singing and to teach a Sunday School class at the Holiness Mission. When an all-day meeting was held, God began to deal with

Martha at the evening service. After much struggle, Martha said a wholehearted yes to God. Still, she didn't feel anything. Some questioned whether she truly had been sanctified. A few days later, a woman from whom Martha sought advice told her to ask God to sanctify her right then and then claim the blessing by faith. She did, but still, nothing.

Another woman spoke of praying all night for the blessing of Pentecost. So Martha did likewise. That night God brought to Martha's mind a man who had wronged her family. She felt God asking her to love her enemy, something she told God she could not do unless God put it in her heart. After that prayer, God cleared her mind and assured her that He had fully come into her life.

Martha remembers the next morning, "The instant I awoke God said to me, 'The King's daughter is all glorious within.'" Then, Martha felt the glory. She continues the story, "Before nightfall of that day, I began to laugh, not loudly, nor boisterously, but in a soft manner. I smiled at everybody I met on the street. . . . This laughing or smiling experience lasted for three months and not only three months, but at intervals has lasted all my life. It was real joy in the Lord." About a year later, Martha felt a call to preach. She told no one, thinking her call was "absurd and ridiculous."

One Saturday evening, Martha was invited to a rescue mission in Boston. After the meeting was opened, the leader unexpectedly turned the service over to Martha. On the spot, she got up and began to speak.

It seemed to me that as I preached I could see sin in the lives of those men, that I could see their ruin and their end. What an agony for their salvation, what a desire to see them saved and transformed possessed me! It gradually took possession of them. And when I gave the altar call, 16 men responded. Some of them were murderers, jail birds, thieves, and renegades of every description. Some of them were out of prison on parole, and some of them lived like rats in holes. . . . It really was a remarkable evening, that Saturday night. That occasion of soul winning made my soul happy.

Some time later Martha was invited by Seth C. Rees, pastor of a Quaker church on Rhode Island, to lead the singing at a camp meeting in Portsmouth. One day, while she walked the grounds, Rees approached her and said, "Martha Curry, thee is to preach this afternoon at three o'clock," and walked away.

Martha went to her tent and cried, pleading with God that she couldn't preach, but when the time came she did.[16] Soon after, another minister approached Martha and handed her the book *Fields' Book on Theology*, saying, "God has called you to preach. You have got the Holy Spirit. Master that book. Then come to me, and I will give you another."

Martha decided to settle the question of whether she was called or not, even if it meant she would again have to pray all night.

> I waited again until the hour was late, closed the doors, shut myself in the dining room below, and went on my knees to talk with God. I spent more than an hour telling Him that I did not know enough to preach, that I did not know how to preach, that I was not capable of preaching, that I was a *Methodist*, and as a woman I would have no opportunity in the denomination of being recognized as a preacher. I begged Him to take away the tormenting thought that I must preach. And every time I paused in my prayer to listen to the voice of God, His only reply to all my excuses was, "Will you preach?"
>
> . . . And with a broken heart, with streaming eyes, I told God if He would give me something from His Word that would make me sure for all time and eternity that it was He who was calling me, and that it was not a notion of mine or of others, I would preach. . . .

I reached up, took the Bible and opened it to these words, "Arise, and speak unto them all that I command thee: be not dismayed at their faces, lest I confound thee before them. For, behold, I have made thee this day a defenced city, and an iron pillar, and brazen walls against the whole land, against the kings of Judah, against the princes thereof, against the priests thereof, and against the people of the land. And they shall fight against thee; but they shall not prevail against thee; for I am with thee, saith the Lord, to deliver thee" (Jeremiah 1:17-19).

As I read these words it seemed that God put the iron pillar down my spine, that He made my forehead like brass, and that He built a wall of defense around me that defended me from everything and everybody that would hinder.

And I could only say, "Amen, Lord! I will preach!"

In early 1902 Martha was ordained an elder in the Association of Pentecostal Churches of America. A report in the March 1902 *Beulah Christian* magazine by A. R. Riggs, pastor of the Lowell, Mass., church declares, "Sister Martha Curry has united with our church and we called a council of churches and ordained her to the ministry. I say, 'God is good to Israel to such as have a clean heart.'"[17] The same magazine reports on one of Martha's recent revivals, "Sister Curry remained the entire week and over the Sabbath after the convention, preaching every night but Saturday. Souls sought salvation at every service."[18]

Martha Curry was not a timid soul. Some of those who attended the church where Martha was ordained and first served as associate pastor and later pastor offer some prize insights into her personality.

One woman who went to hear "Mattie" Curry, as she was known at the Portsmouth camp meeting, recalled, "Someone said, 'she was logic on fire.'" This woman described Martha as "very human and approachable, modest but not extreme either way. She preached[;] she didn't talk. [She was] one of the strongest and most able preachers."[19]

Another woman who had been a little girl in the Lowell church remembers Martha was "very concerned about her flock" and "prayed very forcefully." This woman recalls that some in the church resented Martha "because she was a woman. Men thought she was 'bossy.'"[20] This same woman recalls that after her retirement, Martha returned to Lowell and one day felt led to visit and pray with this woman's sister who was terminally ill. After her visit the sick woman "expressed how happy she was—now that she was right with the Lord. Our family was grateful Miss Curry, our former pastor, obeyed the prompting of the Holy Spirit."[21]

Her obituary offers additional glimpses into her mental capacity, tireless service, and confidence:

> It became evident in her early ministry that she was possessed of extraordinary gifts and talents for the work of the ministry, all of which she employed tirelessly under the anointing of God. Her sermons were marked by a rich content of careful thought, keen insight, loyalty to the Scriptures, and sturdy, inflexible convictions. She was indeed a mighty spiritual leader, one whose leadership it was a joy to follow. Her gift of spiritual discernment was one of her most impressive characteristics. In "trying the spirits" she was rarely deceived.[22]

Martha was pastor of many churches during her 55-year career. Her stay at one of her earliest churches located in Cliftondale, Mass., was cut short due to ill health. After taking a two months' vacation, she did not regain her strength and returned to resign. The minutes of the 10th Annual Meeting of the Association of Pentecostal Churches of America records, "In spite of her illness much seed was sown by Sister Curry in this church and some definite results were obtained."[23]

The pastor of the Cliftondale church contacted Martha 43 years later, inviting her to attend the church's Jubilee

anniversary service or to send an autobiographical sketch
if she couldn't travel. Martha initially declined both requests, but before she mailed her response, she changed
her mind and enclosed an account of her ministry. Written
in shaky longhand as her eyesight was dimming rapidly,
this letter is quoted at length to provide details into her
movements that are otherwise undocumented. Martha ac-
knowledges the lack of dates in her memoir as she was unable to see to look them up.

Left Cliftondale for California and stopped en-route in
Cincinnati and preached every night at the Christian Convention at "God's Bible School," with scores at the altar
seeking and finding salvation and being sanctified. When I
arrived in California, [I] preached in the first church of the
Nazarene in Los Angeles, Dr. Bresee, pastor. From there
went to Ontario, Calif. Had a good revival there with many
souls saved. Then to Berkeley, Calif.—a wonderful meeting
there. Then to Portland, Oregon. We had nearly a hundred
souls then and the nucleus of the church of the Nazarene
was formed. Came back to Washington, D.C. in the Spring
and held a meeting with Chas. H. Davis through a hard
fight, but the church was established, thank God.

My next trip to California I preached in [unreadable lo-
cale] en route. Out of that—and one or two other meetings
held in a tent[—]a church in the Woodlawn District was organized. I served as Pastor for one year at Ontario, California, then resigned and went North and held revivals and
preached at Camp-Meetings. Preached in Spokane, Washington—Walla Walla, Wash., Yakima and Portland, Oregon.
. . . [H]eld that winter five revivals in the city of Portland—
at first church—Sellwood and [Mount School?]. Then came
back East and held revivals all over New England and New
York State. At that time our School in North Scituate, R.I.
got into severe trouble due to a break down in Brother An-
gell's health. The Director asked me to take it—and with
fear and trembling I did. I started a revival and God came
and every member of the School was saved or sanctified,

among them Harold Harding of Malden and his Sister
Hazel, the wife of James Young, Pastor of our church in
Manchester County.

The next year I went to Calif. again and when I came
back took the pastorate of our new church in Ohio. God
gave me a wonderful ministry there, and in two years I took
over 60 members into the church most of whom were converted or sanctified in our church.[24]

I cannot go into any more details,—but I have evange-
lized in nearly all our New England churches. Held three
revivals in our church in So. Portland, Mass., and in Portland church. Two meetings in Malden. One in Everett, and
had a pastorate there. Two in Haverhill—one in Somerville
—Springfield. Preached at Mooers Camp-Meeting. Held a
revival in Saratoga. Have been pastor in Lowell at three different periods. Pastor at Bath, Maine. Have held revivals in
several of our Colleges. Two or three at E.N.C. [Eastern
Nazarene College] in Wollaston. One in Hutchinson, Kansas.[25] One or two in Nampa, Idaho. [Location of Northwest
Nazarene College.]

Have preached at Camp-Meetings and Conventions
with all the pioneers of our church. Dr. Bresee, Dr. Walk-
er—Dr. Reynolds, Dr. Wiley—Dr. Wilson. . . .

In short I am in my 80th year and have lived a full—active and busy life—and God has blessed me—and I praise
Him for it.

My next long journey will be to Heaven and I expect
to share a long eternity with Jesus—who loved me and
washed me in His own blood.[26]

Martha's letter shows the commitment she had to
evangelism, but she was also highly interested in education. In fact, the 1901 minutes of the Association of Pentecostal Churches of America, in documenting the activities
of the Pentecostal Collegiate Institute (predecessor of Eastern Nazarene College) refer to "Miss M. E. Curry, evangelist, who under God has been a true friend and a great help
to the enterprise."[27] Martha is mentioned often in the *Heart*,

Head and Hand, the magazine of the Pentecostal Collegiate Institute, for her "stirring" fund-raising speeches that did much to keep the school open.[28]

Martha Curry's career shows the vigor and commitment that made her one of the few single women ministers who supported herself, eagerly took the challenge of serving churches throughout the country, and used her expansive mental gifts to preach, teach, and evangelize for decades. Martha died in Lowell, Mass., on December 16, 1948, at 81 years of age.

Less than a year before Martha died, a man who visited her home wrote an article "I Meet a Super-Victor," for the *Herald of Holiness.* In it, he wrote that when Martha, who was confined to her home and unable to read, testified to her gratitude for having so much scripture memorized,

> a wonderful light came into her face and her eyes filled with joyful tears. And she told me a strange and beautiful thing. She said that every morning (before arising, if I recall correctly) she repeated to herself 32 hymns she had committed to memory in the long ago!
>
> . . . Going out through the door there was a glow at my heart; I had been in the presence of a "queen unto God," one whose days are full of royal victory.[29]

Surely, this man spoke truly, for Martha lived her life knowing that God had declared on the morn of her sanctification, "The King's daughter is all glorious within."

Olive M. Winchester

Olive Mary Winchester, who was born on November 2, 1879, became a cum laude graduate of Radcliffe Ladies College, a division of Harvard University, in 1902. That year, as Martha Curry conducted a revival at Providence, R.I., she was aided in the preaching by Olive. An account of this series of meetings records that "Sister Olive Winchester, a member of this church, and senior at Radcliffe College, spoke at the morning service with special unction. More than a dozen souls were at the altar."[30] Throughout 1902 Martha Curry and Olive Winchester continued to work together at the Pentecostal Collegiate Institute, traveling the Northeast to raise money for the college while Olive also held services in small communities that lacked regular church services.

In the years following her graduation from Radcliffe, she was the first woman admitted to theological studies at the Divinity School of Glasgow University and the first granted the bachelor of divinity degree in 1912, a feat that took a special resolution of the university trustees. In 1917 she completed an S.T.M. degree from Pacific School of Religion in Berkeley, Calif., and finished with a Th.D. from Drew Theological Seminary in Madison, N.J., in 1925.[31]

Olive, part heiress of the Winchester Rifle estate,[32] financed her own education and generously sponsored theological education efforts throughout her life. She excelled in Latin, Greek, and Hebrew and had a reading knowledge of French and German. Religious education and sociology were two additional fields of study that Olive specialized in, and both were largely learned through personal study and rigorous self-discipline.

While Olive studied in Scotland, she served as an active member of the Pentecostal Church of Scotland. During the Fourth Annual Assembly of the Pentecostal Church of Scotland held in Glasgow on May 10, 1912, Olive, who had just graduated from Glasgow University, preached the Annual Sermon described in the minutes of the assembly as "a scholarly address, based on Daniel 2:34-35." The next day, the minutes record that Olive vigorously advocated that a holiness periodical and college be organized to help perpetuate and strengthen the holiness work in Scotland.

Soon after this discussion it was proposed that Olive be ordained to the ministry, which included the right to "marry, baptize, and dispense the Communion." The minutes record that George Sharpe, the founder of the Pentecostal Church of Scotland, replied to queries raised about the propriety of taking such an action by stating that "as a custom had been broken down in the University when Miss Winchester was admitted, he did not think this church should debar her." When the vote was taken, 21 voted in favor of ordaining Olive, 1 voted against, and 3 abstained.

An undated newspaper clipping shows that the next year, Olive's ministry broke new ground in Scotland as to the ministerial role of women. The clip states,

> At a marriage . . . yesterday, the clergy man who assisted at the ceremony was a lady—the Rev. Olive M. Winchester, upon whom the degree of Bachelor of Divinity was conferred at Glasgow University, two years ago. "Miss Winchester, who is fully qualified by her University career to undertake the ministry of a church, has been ordained by the Pentecostal Church, and is thereby entitled to officiate at a wedding. Yesterday's wedding was the first at which she has assisted, and probably it is the first in Scotland at which a lady minister has officiated."[33]

Correspondence between Olive and H. F. Reynolds proves that she played an influential role in bringing about the union of the Pentecostal Church of Scotland and the Pentecostal Church of the Nazarene in November 1915. She also taught for four years at the fledgling Bible school that arose from the 1912 assembly of the Scottish church.

When Olive returned to the Northeast in 1914, she became vice-principal and head of the Department of Theology at the Pentecostal Collegiate Institute of North Scituate, where she had served from 1902 to 1903 just after completing her studies at Radcliffe. Three years later she moved West to Berkeley, Calif., to attend the Pacific School of Religion.[34]

One of Olive's fellow students at Pacific School of Religion was H. Orton Wiley, the pastor of the Berkeley
Church of the Nazarene. Winchester and Wiley both completed their seminary work in 1917, and Wiley was then
called to be president of Northwest Nazarene College. He
invited Winchester to come and teach at the fledgling college in rural Idaho.

Olive became professor of biblical literature, academic
dean, and later vice president. Her application to teach for
Northwest Nazarene College records that she was converted in 1895 and sanctified in 1902. In answer to the question, "Are you in sympathy with a radical and aggressive
type of holiness work?" an unequivocal yes is penned in
Olive's firm handwriting.[35]

Olive staunchly believed that regeneration and sanctification were instantaneous works of divine grace. In other
theological matters, Olive was an amillennialist, meaning
she rejected the idea of a literal 1,000-year reign before or
after the return of Christ. She also did not see any reason to
ascribe to a literal interpretation of the events described in
the Book of Revelation. She believed that the apocalypse
was intelligible to the readers at the time it was written
and it might have some link to future events, yet outlining
the future was not the author's intent.

Olive was remembered by students and coworkers
alike as a woman of extraordinary strength of character
and scholarship. The documents from "Founders' Day" of
NNC, held September 30, 1966, call Dr. Winchester "the
Founder of the scholastic ideals of Northwest Nazarene
College. She was one of the best trained, best prepared educators in the history of our church." The tribute enumer-
ates Dr. Winchester's personality and gifts.

1. She was a strong personality—very firm but also
   very considerate.
2. She was a person of the highest character, possess-

ing pure integrity, unquestioned courage, and a Scottish will of iron.

3. She was a committed Christian—loyal to Christ, to biblical truth, and to her Church.

4. She was a competent administrator. Details were handled easily, and her department was meticulously organized.

5. In the classroom she was unexcelled; she was an authority in the field of biblical literature. Also, she was a Greek and Hebrew scholar.[36]

Dr. Winchester was a formidable and demanding professor. Students said she could teach two years of Hebrew without ever referring to a dictionary. Thankfully, she also had a sense of humor. Students fondly recall the day she arrived at class preoccupied and harried. She said to the class, "Let us pray," then put her head in her hands as was her custom. She then said, "Our father, we thank thee for this food." When she realized that she had prayed a table grace, she threw back her head and laughed uproariously.

Olive's years at NNC were fraught with financial hardship. Correspondence shows she constantly faced the task of determining which creditors would be paid when scarce funds came into the treasury. In 1934 the bookkeeper's report to the Internal Revenue Service indicates that Olive donated one month's salary ($175) to the college and donated another $200 of her $1,179.16 annual salary to the building fund. She often visited the professors' homes to make sure they had the basic necessities of life and often bought Christmas presents for the faculty children out of her own funds. While lending her financial acumen to the college, for a time she dabbled in the sideline business of raising silver foxes and selling their pelts to New York furriers.

While in Nampa, Winchester loaned President Wiley the funds to build his home. When the college was unable to pay him, he defaulted on his loan. Eventually Wiley and Winchester donated the home to the college, considering it their contribution to Nazarene higher education.

Olive Winchester faithfully served her church through educational and administrative roles. During the 1920s the Church of the Nazarene increased its general support to its educational institutions, taking a strong stand against "worldliness" that resulted in heightened codes of conduct that prohibited undue emphasis on dramatics, competitive sports, and secular music. A highly respected General Board of Education, on which Olive Winchester served for many years, divided the denomination's churches into "educational zones," establishing the principle that each zone was to sponsor only one educational institution. The board also gave official status to schools and colleges with boards of trustees comprised of members of the Church of the Nazarene.

A story recounted by Dr. Ross E. Price, one of Olive's students, illustrates how her sense of calling to the ordained ministry was lived out through contributing to her students. While at Northwest Nazarene College, a portrait of Olive Winchester was commissioned to commemorate her pioneering role at the institution. She accepted the honor with the following words: "I am sending out my students into the stream of life and society. Years from now, away down that River, they will bring ashore my precepts and my teaching. My prayer is that my influence will carry the influence of Christian Ideals learned here at N.N.C. into many a distant port there to bless this and coming generations of humanity."[37]

Olive moved from Idaho in 1935 to join the faculty of Pasadena College where she served as dean of the Graduate School of Religion until her retirement. Students from these years also remember her for her rigorous teaching methods. Olive did not use textbooks. She believed that students learned the most when researching in the library stacks. Each of her syllabi offered questions that the students were required to answer from their library work. The students compiled their answers in card files that Olive believed would make the information most accessible to them in their professional lives.

Olive died in Pasadena on February 15, 1947. One of her students, Harvey B. Snyder, expresses the great impact of her life on the denomination:

> The loss to the college by the passing of Miss Winchester cannot be estimated at this time. She certainly represented a stabilizing influence of no mean proportion. I do not know what provision can be made to provide for her work. . . . Her line of work represented such a type of scholarship that no one to my knowledge in the entire church makes close approach to duplicating it.[38]

Another of the great academics of the early years of the Nazarene church, Bertha Munro, who served as academic dean of Eastern Nazarene College, first encountered Olive at an outdoor meeting at Bertha's girlhood church in Cliftondale, Mass. Later, as a high school student, Bertha visited Olive at Radcliffe and attended a Latin class with her. (Bertha later attended Radcliffe herself.) After her own success in higher education, Miss Munro recalled, "Miss Winchester was a great woman. I always admired her greatly, but it is only with age and experience that I have come to realize something of what the church owes her, and how really she was an intellectual pioneer."[39]

Olive Winchester left $50,000 to Pasadena College for the building of Howard Library. How fitting that even in dying, she left a legacy that would continue her lifelong quest of integrating faith and learning.

A striking characteristic pervades the lives of the New England preachers. Each of the three women ministers began her public ministry as a single woman. Susan Fitkin served as pastor of two churches before marrying. Martha Curry and Olive Winchester remained single throughout their lives. In an era when women's roles were highly defined, these three women exemplify how compelling an inner sense of calling, can be when combined with powerful gifts. All three of these women sought to educate themselves and provide educational opportunities for others. Susan Fitkin helped establish three Bible colleges in Asia and one in South America. Martha Curry steadfastly advocated keeping Pentecostal Collegiate Institute open when it faced great difficulties. Olive Winchester gave her life to the theological training of others. These three believed that training could only help open more doors for those, both men and women, called to the ministry.

4

Women Preachers
in the South

While the union of the Church of the Nazarene with
the Association of Pentecostal Churches of America linked
East and West, the holiness movement in the South developed separately. Claiming a more rural constituency, the
Southern movement viewed the holiness doctrine as a return to "old-time religion." They were not moved by the
optimism characteristic of Northern holiness that heralded
a revolutionized society.

Nazarene Origins in the South

These differences, which showed most in the South's
strong convictions regarding personal ethics, slowed the
formal union between the holiness groups in the North
and South. However, these groups shared most values and
beliefs. As early as 1906, letters were sent from Phineas
Bresee to C. B. Jernigan, the editor of *Highways and Hedges*,
a periodical of the Holiness Church of Christ in the South.[1]
Through such correspondence and regional periodicals,
the holiness groups in all areas of the country kept abreast
of each other's activities.

Representatives of the Holiness Church of Christ were
invited to join in the 1907 discussions of union between the
Church of the Nazarene and the Association of Pentecostal

Churches of America, but finances prohibited any of the Southerners from attending the meeting in Brooklyn. Later that same year, Jernigan and other representatives from the Holiness Church of Christ, including Mrs. E. J. Sheeks, one of the first women ordained in the Southern movement, traveled to Chicago to the General Assembly of the Pentecostal Church of the Nazarene.

By the time delegates met in Chicago, a full union between all three groups had become the main objective. The representatives from the Holiness Church of Christ were placed as delegates on the legislative committee at the General Assembly. Along with them were members from the Church of the Nazarene and Association of Pentecostal Churches in America. Together they helped frame the government and doctrinal statements of a denomination formed by merger. Additions in the Nazarene *Manual* of new articles on the Second Coming and divine healing, along with strengthened statements that "insisted" rather than "advised" members to refrain from joining secret societies or using tobacco, satisfied those Southerners in attendance.

E. J. Sheeks took the news of potential union home to the Eastern Council, and after reading aloud the manuals of the two churches, she made the motion for union. A unanimous decision was followed by much celebration, and the *Manual of the Church of the Nazarene* was immediately put into use by the various congregations of the Eastern Council of the Holiness Church of Christ. The church officers would remain the same until the merger was fully ratified at an upcoming General Assembly scheduled to meet in Pilot Point, Tex., in October 1908.

Upon his return to Texas, Jernigan declared that "holiness of heart and life was made the basis of union, with liberty to all on non-essentials."[2] Jernigan's zeal for the union did not, however, prevent disagreement as to what these nonessentials for members of the church's Western Council

were. The Holiness Church of Christ was a fully congregational organization. Jernigan and others served a role that
was like a superintendency, yet the individual churches, organized into regional councils, maintained great autonomy.

Consequently, when the Western Council of the Holiness Church of Christ voted unanimously for union, the
consensus soon unraveled. A mighty battle raged on what,
exactly, constituted the nonessentials. The Texans requested that the articles in the Holiness Church of Christ's manual pertaining to tobacco and divine healing be substituted
for those negotiated in Chicago. They also requested that
the section of the marriage ritual referring to the exchang-
ing of rings be stricken. These issues were set for debate at
the General Assembly scheduled for October 1908 at Pilot
Point. In the intervening months, Mary Lee Harris Cagle, a
church planter in West Texas and a highly influential
leader, visited Los Angeles and reported that the students
at the Deets Pacific Bible College wore no gold and the
women did not sport short sleeves.

In April 1908 Phineas Bresee, in turn, visited Texas Holiness University in Peniel, Tex. While there, after just four
revival services, Bresee called for the question, Who in attendance would join with the Nazarenes and establish a na-
tionwide denomination committed to holiness? Dr. Edgar P.
Ellyson, the president of the school; his wife, Emily, an ordained minister; the entire faculty; and many students
stepped forward. Bresee quickly organized this group of
103 into a church that appointed Emily Ellyson as their pastor that very night. Apparently, the choice of Emily Ellyson
as pastor was, in part, an intentional act to prove to the Holiness Church of Christ that the Nazarenes were committed
to the ordained ministry of women.[3]

This unexpected turn of events helped expedite the
union between the Holiness Church of Christ and the
Church of the Nazarene.

In October 1908 delegates from both coasts converged in Pilot Point, Tex. The opinions of those from various parts of the country led to heated debate under the large tent. At one point the fight over tobacco and wedding rings led H. D. Brown, district superintendent in the Northwest "to suggest that if union could be had only at the price of multiplying rules the Nazarenes should let the southerners go. His speech, repeated several times, was finally reduced to the words, 'Mr. Chairman, let them go.' Dr. Bresee, his hand upraised, responded each time, 'We cannot let them go, Brother Brown, they are our own folks.'"[4]

A compromise was finally reached. The scriptural references to women's dress from 1 Tim. 2:9-10 were added to the General Rules and minor revisions on tobacco and the dropping of the ring ceremony were finally ratified.

But matters of dress and behavior were not the only subjects of discussion. Many in the Holiness Church of Christ feared that the superintendency used by the Nazarenes would infringe on congregational rights, including who could be ordained. As part of the debate in the Revision of the *Manual* Committee, Mary Cagle insisted that the new *Manual* include an article specifying that the denomination license and ordain women to preach and function in pastoral offices.

Mary's motion advocating a woman's right to preach carried when voted upon, and only then did Bresee speak out:

> [Bresee] proceeded to argue that the ministry of women, like men, was grounded in apostolic privilege and did not require special provision. In his commentary on this episode, [J. B.] Chapman [a future general superintendent], often a defender of women's right to preach and later the husband of an ordained woman, clearly judged Bresee's "gender-neutral" approach to be a stronger case on behalf of women than the "empowerment" approach advocated by Mary.[5]

Mary apparently conceded to this logic although there is no direct statement recorded from her. The fact that both the Holiness Church of Christ and the Church of the Nazarene ordained women, and that Emily Ellyson was officially ordained during the Pilot Point Assembly must have led Mary to concede her strong desire to document a firm denominational stance.

R. Stanley Ingersol, the biographer of Mary Lee Harris Cagle, interprets the ramifications of this act, in light of the decline in women's ministry in the later decades of the denomination:

> Contemporary practice, ritualized, affirmed, and judged secure, led Mary to deny deepest instincts and yield a symbol important for later generations of Nazarene women who would make life-choices in a denomination more conservative in temperament and less committed to the "apostolic" ministry that its founders assumed a settled issue. History confounded Mary's vision and mocked Bresee's judgment that the vitality of female ministry within the Church of the Nazarene had been settled by ample precedent and "apostolicity," and required no distinguishing marks in the church manual.[6]

Mary and the others at Pilot Point were swept up into the desire to create a national holiness denomination. Dr. Bresee's strength of conviction and personality inched the merger ever forward despite the varied demands of the two holiness groups. Bresee and other Northerners, who were advocates of the Spirit as the best guarantee of right behavior, compromised to meet the Southerners who preferred a policy of purity. When all came to agreement, the Church of the Nazarene would henceforth be a church dedicated to a balance between "puritan and perfectionist, between law and liberty."[7]

In the remainder of this chapter we will see how two women, ordained in the decade prior to the merger, lived out these tensions as they sought a place of ministry in the Southern United States.

Mary Lee Harris Cagle

Mary Lee Wasson, a native Alabamian born in 1864 and reared a Methodist, felt a call to the ministry at age 15 and concluded it must be to foreign missions as there would be no opening for such a life in her native land. On sharing her calling with her mother, Mary recalls, "She gave me no encouragement, but on the contrary bitterly opposed me, saying she would rather have me go to my grave than to the foreign field as a missionary."[8]

Five years later during a revival service conducted by Robert Lee Harris, the man she later would marry, Mary felt the Holy Spirit direct that she would not be a foreign missionary but that her work was in her own country. Mary struggled with this revelation and wrote:

> On my face before God, with tears, I would plead to be released. I knew to go out in this country as a woman preacher would mean to face bitter opposition, prejudice, slanderous tongues, my name cast out as evil, my motives misconstrued and to be looked upon with suspicion.
>
> Besides this, I was so conscious of my inability. My educational advantages had been very limited. I was reared a timid, country girl and had never been out in the world—in fact until 27 years of age, had never been outside of my native county in Alabama. It seemed very strange that God would call me when all these things were considered.[9]

Mary couldn't immediately accept her identity as a woman preacher as she had no role models and knew that the social climate of the South would not honor her calling. She determined that she could not preach. Instead she taught school. In 1891 she married Robert Lee Harris, a boisterous, controversial evangelist. The new bride hoped that she could fulfill her calling through marrying a preacher, thus escaping the conviction that she was to preach. For a brief couple of years her strategy worked, yet Robert Lee Harris both encouraged her calling and taught her, by his very style of life, what it meant to live outside of the safe expectations of others.

Robert Lee Harris, ordained a Free Methodist, stirred up people with his strong moralism and disregard for ecclesiastical authority. By 1885 several years before his marriage to Mary, Harris determined to go to Liberia as a missionary. Without going through the proper church channels, he published plans for his African journey and began soliciting funds. He asked for a missionary appointment from the Texas Conference, and after many tried to dissuade him, his request was granted. Although a Free Methodist under missionary appointment, his independent philosophy and manner of operating brought controversy within denominational ranks. Within three years, one of his coworkers died of malaria and others became too sick to continue the work. In the fall of 1888 Harris and his coworkers left Liberia for good. Within a year, he also severed his ties with the Free Methodists. By the time he married Mary, his evangelistic efforts were connected with the Southern Methodists, yet he would always have a dissenting spirit. He never really fit into any category supported by a denominational structure.

Mary traveled with Harris after their marriage and led singing, conducted prayer meetings, and assisted in the overall evangelistic work. As revivals broke out, the Harrises organized independent holiness bands alongside of local Methodist churches, and several such bands emerged in western Tennessee. The Harrises led a tent revival in Milan, Tenn., in 1893 at the request of Donie Mitchum, a Methodist woman professing sanctification. Harris preached his typically strong holiness message. Soon the minister of the local Baptist church where Mrs. Mitchum's husband, a prominent merchant, was an active member, began to rebuff the messages, and the debate between the two ministers was on. The agitation led to great attendance, and the Harrises left Milan well-known.

Robert and Mary Lee Harris soon caught the attention of E. J. and her husband E. H. Sheeks at a nearby revival, and a friendship between the Harrises, Sheekses, and Mitchums flourished. Meanwhile, Robert Lee Harris's unorthodox style led to complaints that he violated church law and created unrest. So in 1893-94 the Memphis Conference and the General Conference of the Southern Methodist church dealt with the problem of itinerant evangelists like Harris by directing individual pastors to conduct their own revivals and to refuse to allow other revivalists to use their church buildings. Only under rare circumstances was an outside evangelist to be invited. This decision did not sit well with Harris.

The following year the Harrises moved to Milan where they had been given a lot to build a home. Soon the Sheekses became business partners in the Mitchums' general store there, and three of the main families that would later bring much of the Southern holiness movement into the Church of the Nazarene had sealed their futures together. By May 1894 Robert left the Southern Methodist church, saying he was no longer willing to fight the institutional obstacles to living out his calling.

Simultaneous to Robert Lee Harris's break with Methodism, he and his wife and their friends embarked upon a second tent revival in Milan. His health during this time became increasingly fragile because he had contracted "consumption of the lungs" during his African sojourn. In order to keep the revival going, he depended on the efforts of various women preachers. For six weeks in the summer three women sent by the World's Missionary Association, a group resulting from a recent schism from the Free Methodists, shared the preaching task.

Robert Lee Harris, his views honed by his early Free Methodist roots, gladly used women preachers. In fact, just three years before, B. T. Roberts, the founder of Free Methodism, had published his tract *Ordaining Women*, a cause he thoroughly backed but was unable to make a tenet of his denomination.

Roberts, in his conclusion, summarized his argument, one that Harris and the earliest preaching women in Milan would have been familiar with:

In the preceding pages the following propositions have been clearly proved.

1. Man and woman were created equal, each possessing the same rights and privileges as the other.
2. At the fall, woman, because she was the first in the transgression, was, as a punishment, made subject to her husband.
3. Christ re-enacted the primitive law and restored the original relation of equality of the sexes.
4. The objections to the equality of man and woman in the Christian Church, based upon the Bible, rest upon a wrong translation of some passages and misinterpretation of others.
   The objections drawn from woman's nature are fully overthrown by undisputed facts.
5. In the New Testament church, woman, as well as man, filled the office of Apostle, Prophet, Deacon or preacher, and Pastor. There is not the slightest evidence that the functions of any of these offices, when filled by a woman, were different from what they were when filled by a man.
6. Woman took a part in governing the Apostolic church. We come, then, to this final CONCLUSION: THE GOSPEL OF JESUS CHRIST, IN THE PROVI-

SIONS WHICH IT MAKES, AND IN THE AGEN-
CIES WHICH IT EMPLOYS, FOR THE SALVA-
TION OF MANKIND, KNOWS NO DISTINCTION
OF RACE, CONDITION, OR SEX, THEREFORE
NO PERSON EVIDENTLY CALLED OF GOD TO
THE GOSPEL MINISTRY, AND DULY QUALIFIED
FOR IT, SHOULD BE REFUSED ORDINATION ON
ACCOUNT OF RACE, CONDITION, OR SEX.[10]

Harris shared B. T. Roberts' views. The two women who would later become ordained ministers, Mary Lee Harris Cagle and E. J. Sheeks, had to struggle between accepting their individual callings, as encouraged by progressives like Roberts, or the opposing opinion that women could not preach publicly, which was deeply ingrained in Southern life and indeed throughout the nation.

The work and writings of Louisa Woosley, the first woman ordained by the Cumberland Presbyterian church in 1889, also influenced the Milan women. Her defense of women, *Shall Woman Preach? Or, the Question Answered*, published in 1891, circulated widely from western Kentucky where Louisa lived to western areas of Tennessee, such as Milan. Also less than a year after the first Milan revival commenced, Susan B. Anthony and Carrie Chapman Catt, leaders of the struggle to open the vote to women, spoke to the Women's Christian Temperance Union of Milan, of which Donie Mitchum was once treasurer. These various influences informed the way the Milan women would perceive their freedoms in ministry.

As the second tent revival in Milan progressed, it became obvious that many in attendance wished to organize an independent local church. Consequently, on July 5, 1894, what later would come to be known as the New Testament Church of Christ was formed.

As could be expected of a church influenced by Robert Lee Harris, congregational autonomy was encouraged. The freedom to call ministers, send missionaries, and discipline members were not to belong to secular relief agencies, and charitable work was to be undertaken from within the church body. The doctrines of holiness, simplicity of dress, and total restraint from alcohol, tobacco, and other opiates were mandated.

During the fall of 1894 it became clear that Robert Lee Harris was dying. Mary was disconsolate, and in her grief locked herself in a room in the Mitchum household to plead with God: "Lord, if you will heal my husband, I will preach; and God answered me with these words: 'Will you do what I want you to do whether I heal your husband or not?' These words came as a thunder clap to my soul."[11]

Mary continued to struggle before God, but finally came to accept her calling, and on November 26, 1894, Robert Lee Harris, who had recently urged his wife to stay in Milan to continue the work after his death, took his last breath. Mary refused to be persuaded by her mother to return to Alabama and determined to stay in Milan and carry on. Committing her energies to building a network of New Testament Churches of Christ, she timidly ventured forth, working with Donie Mitchum or E. J. Sheeks, and visited holiness bands to preach and organize churches. During a revival in Kentucky, Mary was asked to be the featured preacher. Terrified, she consented and for the first time preached with freedom and force. From that day on, no longer was Mary Lee Harris following in her husband's footsteps. She had become a called, confirmed, and powerful preacher in her own right.

One year after Mary began to preach, she traveled to Texas to visit her late husband's relatives. While there, she received requests to speak in a revival in Hillsboro and then to assist in the aftermath of a revival in Swedonia—an immigrant community. Within weeks Mary organized the first New Testament Church of Christ in west Texas, an area that would later become her home and the focus of her ministry for decades to come.

Mary traveled back and forth from Tennessee to Texas frequently over the next three years. A young song evangelist, Annie Johnson, converted in one of Mary's early meetings, became her partner in ministry. In 1896 Mary and Annie toured four counties of west Texas holding revivals. Their work was not easy, as prejudice against women preachers ran high. R. Stanley Ingersol recounts that in Anson, Tex., Mary "encountered strong prejudice against her ministry, with rumors flying that she had abandoned her children and had once operated a bordello."[12] This accusation only served to bolster attendance and prove the deep-seated prejudice and stereotypes women like Mary faced. Folk culture labeled women who spoke publicly as either unfit mothers or prostitutes.

By 1897 Mary spent most of her time in Texas. Annie Johnson had become an evangelist in her own right, and Mary continued organizing new churches with the help of Trena Platt, a song evangelist who became her primary companion for four years.

In 1898-99 Mary served her first pastorate in Mulberry Canyon, Tex., a church she had earlier organized.

As congregations affiliated with the New Testament Church of Christ increased, so did the need for clergy to tend them. On December 12, 1899, the first congregational meeting of the Milan New Testament Church of Christ essentially became a denominational business meeting, as many of the evangelists and workers in the movement held their membership in the Milan church.

During this gathering the issue of ordaining women rose to the fore. The first day the discussion was raised and tabled. The next day it was deemed that women were entirely eligible for ordination. That very afternoon Mary Lee Harris and E. J. Sheeks applied to the congregation for ordination, and on December 14, 1899, at 9 A.M., they were ordained.

The ordination of Mary Lee Harris and E. J. Sheeks forged the way for many other women called to the public ministry. When the New Testament Churches of Christ documented their *Government and Doctrines* in 1903, one of the eight points deemed essential to put in writing was women's right to preach. Item 7 states, "We believe that women have the same right to preach the gospel as men have." The document then lists Luke 2:36-38; Phil. 4:3; Acts 21:9; 2:17-18; and Rom. 16:1 as scriptural proof.[13] Is it any wonder, then, that five years later Mary Lee Harris would put her energies behind trying to have a similar statement inserted into the *Manual of the Church of the Nazarene?*

A week after her ordination, Mary moved permanently to Buffalo Gap, Tex. Eight months later, on August 8, 1900, during the Buffalo Gap camp meeting, she married Henry Cagle, a pastor in the movement who had been converted under her preaching in 1897. This twosome worked together in ministry for the next 50 years. Mary was 10 years older than Henry and by far the better preacher, while he proved to be the more able administrator.

Domestic duties did not hinder Mary's ministry. She and Trena Platt continued on the revival circuit soon after the wedding as Henry enrolled in Texas Holiness University. Her relocation to Texas and her marriage to Henry Cagle, which friends in Milan did not support, signaled Mary's new sense of independence. She indeed had founded and nurtured the New Testament Church of Christ in Texas. In 1902 Mary instigated the formation of the Western Council of the New Testament Church. No longer would the Milan church determine the future of the Texas congregations. William E. Fisher became president of the Western branch, and Mary chaired the Committee on the State of the Church. She also served on the committees that considered candidates for ordination and oversaw the educational work of the council.

Two years later, the New Testament Church of Christ merged with the Independent Holiness church. During the next year, Fannie McDowell Hunter, a Kentucky evangelist, edited the volume titled *Women Preachers* that gave a biblical defense for women's right to preach and documented the call of nine women preachers. Seven of the women came into the new Holiness Church of Christ with the New Testament Church of Christ. Johnny Jernigan was the eighth woman featured, and as the wife of C. B. Jernigan, she proved that both of these merging groups shared the belief in ordaining women to full ministerial status.

In order to get a full glimpse into the influence these women held in the Holiness Church of Christ, R. Stanley Ingersol cites the following facts:

> Of the sect's 156 ordained elders in December 1906, there were 13 clergy couples. Another 10 women, either single, or like E. J. Sheeks, married to a non-clergy spouse, were on the roll. Thus, nearly one of every six ordained elders was female, and nearly one in every four was either a woman minister or her spouse. Of 49 licensed preachers, five were women. Seven of eight authorized, (evangelists or home missionaries) were women, while six of 12 ordained (foreign) missionaries were. These figures do not take into account female lay preachers like Donie Mitchum who at various times evangelized and served as pastors.[14]

Mary continued as evangelist and church planter with her husband during the brief years the Holiness Church of Christ existed before its union with the Pentecostal Church of the Nazarene in 1908. After becoming a Nazarene, Mary's role shifted as her informal superintendency of the dozen or so churches she organized was placed under the jurisdiction of a district superintendent according to Nazarene polity. For the next four decades Mary essentially served as an evangelist yet took an occasional pastoral charge. In 1908 she oversaw four churches—Hamlin, Swedonia, Mount Zion, and Roby—as pastor. The next year she and Henry organized and served as copastors of a church in Lubbock after five years of traveling over 200 miles to hold annual revivals there.

Eight years later Henry Cagle was elected as district superintendent of the New Mexico District. During Henry's two-year term, Mary was district evangelist, a role that carried the responsibility of building up existing churches and paving the way for new congregations. During the following two-year period, 1921-22, the Cagles served in similar capacities on the Arizona District while Mary took on the additional task of ministering to the Peoria, Ariz., church. The Hamlin District then called them home to Texas where Henry was district superintendent and Mary district evangelist from 1926 to 1931, yet here in familiar territory, their roles looked more like cosuperintendents.

Mary's report to the 1927 District Assembly shows how the couple worked together:

> Our work has not been with the larger churches, but with the weak, struggling ones. I have held 13 revival meetings, preached 175 times, saw 216 converted and 118 sanctified, and . . . have travelled about 10,000 miles in a car and have made a few trips on the train. I have [visited] practically all of the churches in the district and some of them more than once. Have done the heaviest part of the correspondence; as my husband has been on the go nearly all the time, it was impossible to keep the mail up with him, so I have tried to keep it up with me.[15]

Precarious health befell Mary soon after this exhausting year, and the Cagles exited administrative roles and resumed evangelistic efforts as their primary profession for the remainder of their lives.

Yet Mary always found time to be involved in district challenges, often serving on various influential committees, such as Orders and Relations, Church Extension, and the District Advisory Board. During six General Assemblies she was elected as a clergy delegate and served on the *Manual* Revision committee.

As Mary aged, she lost none of her desire to preach or her conviction to agitate for women's rights to preach. In 1939, when sent a standard form for clergy that only used male pronouns, she returned it blank. She inquired how she was to complete it, "when the blanks are only for men?"

Correspondence between Mary and the general secretary of the Church of the Nazarene in 1938 helps to summarize how Mary remained faithful to God's call upon her life to her last days on earth. In discussing her eligibility for the church's pension plan she writes to Fleming, "What you said about grace to retire gracefully struck me. . . . We are queer creatures anyway. I almost had to know that it was preach or hell before I would do it, and now when the time is nearing when I will have to quit, the thought of it nearly breaks my heart."[16]

Mary is documented as retiring in 1942, but she is listed as evangelist and pastor in various locales over the next six years. Blind and infirm, she preached on February 4, 1954, her 90th birthday, held up by two friends as she delivered her final, rousing half-hour sermon. Mary Cagle, outstanding church pioneer and crusader, died on September 27, 1955.

Elliott J. Sheeks

Elliott J. Doboe entered the world as the second of nine children born to a Kentucky farm family on January 8, 1872. She experienced a spiritual conversion at the age of 11 and joined the Cumberland Presbyterian church.

Several years later, at the age of 17, E. J. attended a revival service and first encountered the holiness doctrine. The initial sermon convicted her and led her to a recommitment from a "backslidden condition."

Soon after this revival, E. J. received a request to lead a prayer meeting. She resisted, and in her own words explains why she was so reluctant: "Previous to this time I had never prayed in public nor conducted a public service. Not only was it the teaching of the denomination to which I belonged that women must keep silence in the Church and must not speak in public, but my mother was bitterly opposed to women speaking in public. I was 14 years of age before I ever heard a woman pray in public."[17]

E. J. did lead the prayer meeting and as soon as it concluded, her sister, who had attended, told their mother who strongly objected and forbade E. J. to ever do such a thing again. E. J. went to her room and prayed until she was comforted.

Since early childhood E. J. had felt she was to give her best efforts to God and assumed that she was to be a missionary. She eagerly read every account she could of those who served overseas. She "did not think that a woman would be allowed to preach the Gospel here in Christian America."[18]

At the age of 18 E. J. heard a woman preach for the first time. Louisa Woosley conducted a camp meeting near E. J.'s home, and she attended with her mother. E. J. recalls that after hearing Woosley preach, her mother "was convinced that a woman under the leadership of the Holy Ghost had the right to preach or speak in religious services. Many times since have I heard her pray, testify, and even shout the praises of God."[19]

How freeing this event must have been for E. J. when her own call to preach was clarified. Her inner conviction that she was to preach despite opposition was confirmed by the knowledge that there were women preachers. She had heard Louisa Woosley preach powerfully in the face of great trials.

In her late teens E. J. met E. H. Sheeks, a successful salesman more than 30 years her senior who worked for G. I. Neptune Hard Barrel Stave Company. Before her 20th birthday, on October 4, 1891, E. J. married this man who was well-educated from Asbury College and wealthy in experience as he had served in the Civil War and had already completed one career in the hotel industry.

The couple moved to Memphis where E. J. attended the Old State Female College. The Sheeks joined the Methodist church and E. J. busied herself with church work and, by her own account, keeping up with others in fashion and luxurious living. While living in Memphis, the Sheeks attended a tent revival held by Robert Lee Harris. His searing sermons denouncing worldly living convicted E. J. and she committed herself wholly to God.

This connection with the Harrises led the Sheekses to move to Milan, Tenn., where they became charter members of the New Testament Church of Christ, although it was unclear if E. H. Sheeks would join at one point. His wife recollected her own dilemma at joining in a retrospective letter sent to Donie Mitchum some 35 years later:

> For we discussed the matter quite a lot at home, and we could not get Mr. Sheeks to commit himself on the subject, and I had quite a test in making up my mind to join unless he joined also. But we women [E. J. and the women evangelists from the World's Missionary Association] all agreed that we would go into the organization. I well remember that when Brother Harris gave the opportunity for all to come forward who wanted to go into the organization, that, with fear and trembling, I arose and went forward, wondering what Mr. Sheeks would do, when lo and behold! he came also.[20]

Two years after meeting the Harrises, E. J. claimed the experience of entire sanctification in her own room while reading a collection of sermons by John Wesley. That night she vowed to do anything God would ask of her, including going to India.

But God called E. J. specifically to preach soon thereafter, and she resisted. She was willing to lead prayer meetings, jail services, and speak to the local rescue home for girls, but she feared that following a call to preach would mean "sacrifice, self-denial, reproach, opposition and persecutions." In her worst imaginings she might lose her comfortable home and supportive husband. One night, all night, she prayed and argued with God and finally prayed, "Lord, if it takes husband and everything else on earth, I'll preach, for I am assured the call is from Thee."[21] She then told her husband of her calling. E. H. Sheeks didn't mind a bit. In fact, he bought her a tent to house her meetings. Shortly, thereafter, E. J. began her public work as song evangelist for Mary Lee Harris, and in a revival in Monett, Ark., she preached her first sermon.

After Robert Lee Harris' death, E. J. worked with Mary Lee Harris and Donie Mitchum as the three women carried the work of the New Testament Church of Christ throughout the area surrounding Milan. As Mary's focus became west Texas, and Donie's four young children and their needs restricted her to local travel, E. J. inherited much of the task of holding revivals and organizing churches in Tennessee, Arkansas, and Mississippi.

In 1901 E. J. wrote several letters to the Mitchum family that give an idea of her flurry of activity. During a recent camp meeting at Beebe, Ark., eight churches had asked E. J. to either hold meetings or take pastoral charge, but she already was giving one Sunday a month to the Hillville church, where she served for nine years, and another Sunday to Stony Point where there were 36 members "and more to follow." During a revival at Stony Point, Ark., E. J. records that "over a hundred [were] converted or sanctified, most of them young people and a number who had lived in sin to middle age and were what they call 'hard cases.'"[22] She no doubt anticipated bringing many of those into church membership.

Her activities kept her on the road a great deal. At the 1904 Annual Council she reported traveling 7,600 miles and preaching 182 sermons. The *Pentecostal Herald* records her summer evangelistic slate for 1904 as follows:

Banner, Miss., July 1-10

Luray, Tenn., July 14-24

Hillville, Tenn., July 28—Aug. 7

Stony Point, Ark., Aug. 14-24

Roby, Tenn., Aug. 23—Sept. 7

Black Oak, Ark., Sept. 15-25[23]

E. J.'s schedule was kept full in part because she was known as a straightforward preacher. When she traveled to Banner that summer she found the town to be "the deadest and most prejudiced place I ever saw. Before I begun the meeting, many said they would have nothing to do with the meeting and called me a heretic."[24] Apparently the lack of welcome E. J. received did nothing to deter her. One attender at the 1904 revival in Banner, Miss., offers a compliment to her power as a preacher: "Permit me to say that when you want the pure gospel, the whole-gospel that makes no compromise with sin, that demands an immediate surrender to God by the sinner and lead[s] the justified to a higher attainment in the Christian religion, just send for Mrs. E. J. Sheeks."[25]

E. J. combined the holiness message with strong notions of personal piety. In retelling the story of one girl "rescued" in Little Rock in 1905, E. J. says that as she walked the girl back to the Crittenton Home after the service, the girl was under conviction for her worldliness and pride. When they arrived at the home, the girl ripped the silk skirt she wore in two and then went inside and gathered up all of her "fine clothes" and took them to the back-yard and burned them. "This girl literally burned up everything she had in a life of sin, even to her shoes and toilet articles. And the hand of God is on her for His service. She has gifts and abilities and is now in training school preparing for the work of the Lord."[26]

In 1907, after serving her Stony Point charge for seven years, E. J. resigned her pastorate to become chair and lecturer on rescue work for the Arkansas Holiness Association. Two years earlier E. J. had called for the Eastern Council of the Holiness Church of Christ to establish a rescue home in Arkansas. She raised funds and interest enough to help buy a piece of land for the home in Little Rock, but the venture eventually failed. She continued to advocate for rescue work until 1910, when the Nazarene Hope Cottage was established in Texarkana. For many years she served on the board of directors of the home.

In the third decade of her ministry E. J. concentrated her energies on serving the Arkansas and Dallas districts as district secretary. In 1915 she enrolled in Peniel College, formerly Texas Holiness University, and graduated from the "Greek-Theological Course" the next year. She and her husband, who was now retired, moved to Hutchinson, Kans., in about 1925 where she became a member of the faculty of Bresee College. During the summers she enrolled in Sterling College and earned a bachelor's degree in theology.

In a 1935 letter to Donie Mitchum, E. J. tells her friend of her busy teaching life:

> Am teaching 18 hours a week at the college and am teaching by extension, World History, American History, Psychology, Ethics, Missions, N.T. History, Homiletics, Hermeneutics, Syst. Theology, English IV, Constitution, Pastoral Theology. The pupils taking the above subjects come here and take private lessons at night or in the after-

noons after school hours. Then I am teaching by correspondence: Systematic Theology, Missions, Church History.[27]

E. J. suffered the loss of her husband in 1939 when he was 96 years old. The following year she had a stroke and was forced to curtail many of her activities. She died in 1946, leaving behind a great legacy of evangelism, rescue work, and learned pupils. She and her husband had one son, John.

The women of the South who started and brought so many churches into the Church of the Nazarene also brought with them a commitment to sisterhood that enabled them to minister in a difficult social milieu. They knew strength could be found in numbers.

Mary Lee Harris Cagle tried to find a culturally acceptable way to channel her call to preach by working under the leadership of her first husband. His encouragement to speak out was essential to her accepting her calling, and his death galvanized her to act. She had also heard the public preaching of women evangelists from the World's Missionary Society. She knew others who shared her unusual calling. The support of those closest to her helped Mary find her voice. If she hadn't, the movement might not have flourished. It is not surprising that she held her evangelistic meetings jointly with other women ministers. Donie Mitchum and E. J. Sheeks shared the platform with her in the earliest days. Annie Johnson Fisher and Trena Platt worked alongside Mary during the four-year period when she pushed the New Testament Church of Christ into town after town in west Texas.

E. J. Sheeks also tried to squelch her calling by throwing herself into church work. She feared losing all—her husband, home, reputation—if she dared comply with the Spirit's leading her to preach. Once she settled the question for herself, her husband's support and the Milan sisterhood propelled her onward.

These women relied on the encouragement of like-minded women ministers as they fulfilled their individual callings. Perhaps that is one reason they accomplished so much despite the pervading cultural opinions that could have stopped them at any point along their faithful journeys.

5

Women Preachers in the Southeast

Small holiness groups from all sectors of the country continued to join with the Church of the Nazarene for decades to come. The last large group, the Pentecostal Mission of Nashville, united on February 14, 1915, after eight years of negotiation.

J. O. McClurkan and the Church of the Nazarene in the Southeast

The Pentecostal Mission arose as a loose organization of holiness groups in middle Tennessee. J. O. McClurkan, the founder, was a native of Tennessee who returned to Nashville in 1897 after a two-year revival trek across the country from California where he had served as a Cumberland Presbyterian minister. McClurkan claimed the experience of sanctification after attending a Methodist revival in San Jose, Calif., in 1895.

Although McClurkan did not intend to stay in Nashville, his son's poor health, as well as his own, caused him to prolong a very successful tent meeting he was holding, and by the end of the summer of 1897, McClurkan was sought out as a leader for the holiness people of the area. A new vision of how he could enable the efforts of the holiness bands and associations germinated in his mind, and in 1898 a committee began working on how to organize these groups without forming a new denomination.[1]

For the next 17 years the Pentecostal Mission supplied a network of local holiness groups in which people would form a local Pentecostal Mission belonging to a district with ministerial supervision. Membership was never required, but professed faith and active involvement in the local missions made one a part of the organization.

In addition to providing a backbone for the holiness movement in Tennessee, the Pentecostal Mission made a strong commitment to foreign missions. Throughout the duration of the Pentecostal Mission, work began in Cuba, Central America, South America, and India. The overseas work was most dear to McClurkan's heart and a prime reason that the Pentecostal Mission and the Christian and Missionary Alliance, a staunch mission-minded denomination, were closely aligned for several years.

This zeal for missions spawned the development of a Bible training school for missionaries that McClurkan later named Trevecca College. It exists today as Trevecca Nazarene College.

As the Pentecostal Mission grew, J. O. McClurkan recognized the need for additional organization, although he resisted the idea of forming a new denomination. In 1905 representatives from the Pentecostal Mission attended the Arkansas Council of the Holiness Church of Christ to discuss a merger. However, the Holiness Church of Christ was already moving toward joining forces with the Pentecostal Church of the Nazarene.

The two Southern holiness groups already cooperated informally with each other. Some members of the Holiness Church of Christ sent monetary support to the missionaries sponsored by the Pentecostal Mission and penned articles of interest to holiness people in the Southeast for *Zion's Outlook* (later titled *Living Waters*), the organization's newspaper. Further contact was enhanced when R. B. and Donie Mitchum moved to Nashville in 1906 and attended the Nashville Tabernacle where McClurkan served as pastor.

Evidently knowing the Holiness Church of Christ would likely merge with the Nazarenes, McClurkan turned his sights toward the possibility of joining as well. He wrote to Phineas F. Bresee on January 1, 1907, expressing the need to turn the local missions into churches so that they might continue for years to come. McClurkan acknowledged that uniting with the Nazarenes would only come after certain negotiations. In that first letter he registered his objections to the length of the denominational name along with desire to have the foreign missionary work of the denomination located in Nashville. The only letter reply in existence from Bresee doesn't counter these issues as he did not see them as problems. The concerns in his letter refer to doctrinal issues that must have been raised in other correspondence. Bresee states that agreement on doctrine should be "simple" and "essential." "Nonessentials" should be left to "personal liberty." Bresee believed that Christians could hold different opinions on various issues and still be holy people. Tolerance was necessary, and fussing about "nonessentials" was counterproductive.

Only when delegates from the Pentecostal Mission arrived at Pilot Point in 1908 did the points of doctrinal contention become clarified. The issues of premillennialism and the ordination of women stifled the possibility of union. The Pentecostal Mission saw much of its work as "11th hour" efforts. Their premillennial view of the second coming of Christ led them to focus on evangelism and missions as they saw the world as an increasingly wicked and ungodly place. As the world got worse, Jesus would return to claim the faithful. The mandate then was to increase the ranks of the faithful through any means possible.[2] This seems to have been the operative philosophy in the Pentecostal Mission, until the growing numbers of local missions simply mandated further structure.

The issue of ordaining women was not open to compromise. All three groups that had previously merged to form the Pentecostal Church of the Nazarene had ordained women. McClurkan's group allowed women to work as teachers, missionaries, and evangelists but did not ordain them, and McClurkan believed women could speak publicly but were spiritually prohibited from "ruling positions."

The impasse on these issues caused the Pentecostal Mission to opt for strengthening its internal organization rather than joining the Nazarenes. Annually for seven years the question of uniting with the Nazarenes was reopened, but no agreement was ever made. Finally, McClurkan encouraged the Pentecostal Church of the Nazarene to organize its own churches in middle Tennessee and Kentucky. When they responded by doing so, many of the members of local Pentecostal Missions joined the Nazarenes and provided the backbone of its separate efforts. In 1913 McClurkan's wife, Martha Frances Rye McClurkan, addressed the Clarksville, Tenn., District Assembly of the Church of the Nazarene, and her husband shared the pulpit with Phineas Bresee, but the organizations remained separate.

Two coinciding crises moved the Pentecostal Mission ever closer to the Nazarenes. The foreign mission work was in debt, as was Trevecca College. The loose structure of the Pentecostal Mission made raising funds increasingly difficult as the monetary need grew. Then McClurkan became very ill with typhoid. As he took to his deathbed, his wife asked what he wanted done with the mission. He replied that they should unite with the Nazarenes.

McClurkan died on September 16, 1914, and within

weeks the details of union were being negotiated. On February 15, 1915, the Nazarenes assumed responsibility for the missionary work but would only guarantee the continuation of the work in India as it was well established. Each local mission group was free to join the larger denomination if it so desired. The credentials of all ministers were recognized, and all property belonging expressly to the Pentecostal Mission was transferred to the Nazarenes. The representatives of the Pentecostal Mission declared themselves in agreement with the *Manual* of the Pentecostal Church of the Nazarene, and the issues of premillennialism and women's ordination remained unchanged and ceased to be cause for dissent.

Documenting the significant role women played in the Pentecostal Mission is more difficult than in the other regional bodies as the women's work was mostly carried on unofficially. The lists of evangelists licensed in the 17-year duration of the Pentecostal Mission show that 39 percent were women. Preaching women undergirded the work of the Pentecostal Mission, but sadly many of their contributions are lost to us.

Frances Rye McClurkan

We do know that Martha Frances McClurkan, wife of J. O. McClurkan, preached regularly during her husband's ministry. Their daughter, Merle McClurkan Heath, recounted her father's attitude toward her mother's preaching:

> My father believed that a preacher should be able to preach at any time. He felt the same about my mother. And so it was that a timid country girl became, under the power of the spirit, and of my father, a flaming witness for God from coast to coast, on the street, in jails and slums, in tent or pulpit. No one enjoyed her messages more than he. He always felt a very special need of her presence in an altar

service, often calling upon her to exhort or pray, or to lead some soul to Christ.[3]

The McClurkans were married on November 15, 1882, in Frances's home in Yellow Creek, Tenn. J. O. had just recovered from an extended illness, and his health had been frail since boyhood. On their wedding day, Frances's father said to his daughter, "I'm tellin' you, Frances, Jim McClurkan won't live a year."

"'I'll show him,' she stubbornly purposed in her heart. 'If anything happens to Jimmie, I'll paddle my own canoe.'"[4]

Frances and J. O. left the day they were married to claim a Cumberland Presbyterian pulpit in Decatur, Tex. After two years there, J. O. felt compelled to go to California. The family did just that, and J. O. McClurkan served a pastorate at Visalia and Selma before being sent to San Jose, where the church had been deserted and locked up. McClurkan began his "doorstep ministry," as he took block after block and began to visit each home inviting those who didn't have a church to worship at his.

During this time, a woman stopped Frances as she was leaving the church one day and asked if she had attended the holiness meetings held at the Methodist church where the preacher's sermons were "deeply satisfying." Merle McClurkan Heath recounts the story her mother told her children of that day:

> Here the woman's hands fluttered and lay on her breast motionless in symbol of an inner "peace that passeth all understanding."
>
> Mother often told us that as she stood there listening to this woman she felt as if she were looking into a pool of clear, cool water. Then she was thirsty, thirsty for something she did not have, thirsty for something she knew not what. All at once she realized that her one desire was to attend this meeting.[5]

That night J. O. was late in coming home, and they missed

the revival service. Frances was in tears from disappointment. But the next night they arrived on time, and the preaching on the experience of sanctification captivated J. O. Frances worried that this was fanaticism. Would this new doctrine hinder J. O.'s already effective ministry? So out of fear she determined to take the family out of town the next day, which she did. But by afternoon J. O. announced he was going to catch the next train home so he could attend that evening's service. Frances decided she, too, would go, and that night J. O. accepted the blessing of sanctification. Frances recalled, "He seemed to be aglow with a radiance that made me feel black as a ball of pitch."[6]

Several days later Frances, too, claimed sanctification and felt a great joy, and the next day, Sunday, J. O. called her forward to testify. Her verve and eloquence "swept that congregation like a breath from heaven."[7] The official board found alarming the fervor that arose as other church members claimed sanctification. They also disapproved of a woman speaking publicly. The ruling elder in the church asked the questions, "What are we going to do with Mrs. McClurkan's testimony?"

Soon after claiming a second blessing experience, J. O. went out of town, and Frances began to doubt her sanctification. For several days she did not sleep or eat. Then one day she heard the sound of footsteps in the hallway. J. O. had come home early. Was he sick? No, he had simply felt impressed to return home to give his wife a copy of the book *The Christian's Secret to a Happy Life* by Hannah Whitall Smith. Frances read the book and conquered her doubts.

Soon the McClurkans headed back to Tennessee for a visit, but the trip home soon became an evangelistic tour that lasted two years. As the family traveled by train, stopping to conduct revivals, J. O. often called his wife forward to give a word of testimony after the opening songs. When she finished, J. O. extended the altar call, in effect making Frances the one to lead the service.

In Charlotte, Tenn., nearing the end of this evangelistic sojourn, J. O. asked his wife to officially speak and lead the service. She responded, "Speak! Why I would not have the least idea what to say." Her husband, well knowing her fervent prayers, advised, "Just say on your feet the things you say on your knees."[8]

Frances did, and from that time on she took charge of children's services and afternoon services. Once, during a large camp meeting in Texas, she was in charge of the overflow services, and from an improvised pulpit, Frances spoke in the open air. Because of her commanding physical appearance and full voice, and that intangible virtue of presence, she came to be known as one of the best open-air speakers in the work of the Pentecostal Mission.

In 1920, six years after her husband's death, Dr. H. F. Reynolds requested that Frances be ordained as an elder in the Church of the Nazarene.

Frances McClurkan lived the remainder of her 101 years in Nashville and was highly involved in the lives of the students at Trevecca College. An obituary from the weekly paper of Nashville First Church of the Nazarene, which she attended until her death on June 17, 1966, reports, "Active unto the end . . . She kept abreast of the times. She was aware of the religious movements and events of our day. Recently she had some pointed comments on the 'God is Dead' theory, showing that she was vitally interested in all that pertained to God and the Church."[9]

Frances McClurkan deserves a great place in Nazarene history for the partnership role she played in the early years of the Pentecostal Mission. Still, there were many other women who served as ministers in the Southeast. The lives of two other women ministers help to show the diverse and essential roles women played in the movement.

Leila O. Stratton is perhaps the most accessible of preaching women that joined with the Nazarenes, and Leona Gardner is certainly one of the earliest missionaries. It is to their stories that we now turn.

Leila Owen Stratton

Leila Owen Stratton lived her entire life in the South. She was born in Talbotton County, Ga., on August 16, 1863. Converted in childhood and married at the age of 23 she moved to Lebanon, Tenn., in 1885 with her new husband. While Leila was a new mother (she eventually would give birth to four daughters), she experienced sanctification. By 1902 she had already been in evangelistic work for some time in the area surrounding her home.

In 1903 a tabernacle bearing the name Pentecostal Mission was erected 16 miles from Lebanon. The hall, built to seat 400 worshipers, was full to overflowing during the eight nights of revival services that followed the dedication on the first Sunday of October. Leila and her coworker, Mrs. William Martin, followed up these services, where it is presumed that Leila presided, by visiting biweekly prayer meetings in the various neighborhoods surrounding the new tabernacle.[10]

During the same year another tabernacle was built at Wilford, also known as Stratton's Corner. Leila held a revival at Stratton's Corner in August 1908, and an attender at the revival registered this report: "I am glad to report a real good meeting. Sister L. O. Stratton did the preaching. The meeting began on the first Sunday in August and continued nine days . . . Sister Stratton was at her best. She knows the truth and makes it plain to all who give her their attention."[11]

As the local mission grew, an increased need for organization was expressed. Consequently, on October 23,

1908, several weeks after the revival, "Deacons and Deaconesses were elected, Mrs. Stratton being called to the special care and general oversight of the work." The group already with a good number of members, chose to call itself the "Christian Union at Stratton's Corner" and invited "Christians of all churches, and of no church to fellowship with us."[12] From all evidence it seems clear that Leila was pastor to this group. McClurkan's objections to women in "ruling positions" does not seem to have been held by all of the local mission units. Leila Owen Stratton clearly was in charge of the work in both the Lebanon and Stratton's Corner tabernacles.

Documents concerning Leila's work are not easy to come by. Her reports in *Living Water* indicate a desire to deflect attention from herself. She seems to have been a highly relational woman who had to restrain herself from writing down all the names of those who helped her in revivals or those who received help. One account in the September 1, 1904, issue of *Living Waters* recounts a revival held at the Stratton's Corner tabernacle. "Our dear sister L. O. Stratton held this blessed meeting. She says she don't [sic] like for her name to be put in the papers, I will take the liberty to use it this time, she did all the preaching. We love her so much for bringing this sweet message to us."[13]

In August of 1910 Leila took what she thought was a vacation to visit her sisters in Georgia, but invitations to preach at the local Methodist church and the church of her girlhood awaited her. She preached sanctification amid many relatives and then traveled on to Florida to hold meetings. Leila then recorded that she would "return to Tennessee soon, then for a week at Baltimore, a month or six weeks in Louisiana, and then—and then—well, He knows, and His servants love and serve Him."[14] Leila went where called and guided the local tabernacles when home.

Although her actual contributions to the organization

at large are unknown, Leila became one of the best-known women preachers associated with the Pentecostal Mission. At the 1912 Annual Convention, she addressed the gathered delegates, and when J. O. McClurkan became bedridden it is recalled that, "dear Sister Stratton, a mighty woman of prayer, appeared to the anxious, waiting Pentecostal people, telling them to worry no more, for the answer had come to her that Brother McClurkan would surely recover."[15] McClurkan did not recover, yet it is important to note that Leila was called to bring comfort to the people at large. This shows the extent of her influence.

A few years after joining with the Nazarenes, Leila Stratton gave her energies to the Women's Christian Temperance Union. Known throughout her career as a "strict prohibitionist," she traveled extensively through the South as a national organizer and served as the vice president of the WCTU for the State of Tennessee.

In 1922 she moved to Miami, Fla., presumably after the death of her husband as he is not mentioned after that, and it is recorded that he died many years before she did. References are made to her evangelistic efforts among the Miami churches until her death nearly 17 years later in 1938 at the age of 74.

Leona Gardner

While Leila Owen Stratton exemplified the way women used their gifts in a Pentecostal Mission through evangelistic work, Leona Gardner complimented her efforts in middle Tennessee by showing the ways women undergirded the missionary efforts that were so dear to J. O. McClurkan's heart.

Leona Gardner was born the daughter of a minister of the Methodist Episcopal Church South near Franklin, Tenn., in 1868. Early in life she aided her parents in their evangelistic efforts by working in revival efforts and teaching the Bible class for adults, both men and women, who were older than she.

The doctrine of holiness was not a part of Leona's experience until a female cousin visited her family from Illinois. This unnamed cousin shared her new faith experience with her relatives. Leona remembers:

> In the social conversation with our family that afternoon, I felt the influence of her life calling me into seeking after the same kind of an experience that she had. Consequently after they returned to their home I wrote her about my desire to obtain the experience. Her husband, Dr. Stoddard, wrote me in reply, encouraging me to continue seeking. He sent me many copies of *The Christian Witness*. These I studied diligently. My father had *Binny's Theological Compendium* and *Mrs. Hester Ann Rogers*[16] among his books so I read them diligently and studied the Bible references of the former. So day by day my hunger increased. I prayed and sought day and night. Sometimes I dreamed that I had received sanctification, but when I woke I found it to be only a dream. I sought secretly. I did not want my father nor others to know that I was seeking what they considered heresy.[17]

Leona's seeking was soon to be rewarded as a holiness revival came to Franklin. Several local ministers experienced sanctification, including the pastor of Leona's little country church, who then led Leona into the "final step of consecration." Within hours she spoke publicly of her experience. In her words she writes, "The next day in a testimony meeting God poured out His Spirit upon me abundantly. O what a blessed memory! I was the first witness to this work in the Church in the community where I lived."

Two years later Leona felt called to "the work of evangelism as a helper to others." The woman evangelist whom she assisted soon took her to Nashville and "placed [her] under the care of Bro. and Sis. McClurkan who were then in their first tent campaign in that city." Two years later Leona felt a definite call to the mission field and enrolled briefly in Trevecca College. "I then thought it would be to the savage Indians of North America. I thought that I could not learn a foreign language and that as many of them I thought could speak English I could work among them. I offered myself to the Pentecostal Mission for foreign work."

The Pentecostal Mission sent its first missionaries abroad in 1901 to Central America. The next year Mr. and Mrs. John L. Boaze and Leona Gardner were accepted for missionary work among the Indians in Colombia. They set sail in January of 1902, but severe storms and internal revolution prohibited entry into Colombia, so the group landed in Trinidad, Cuba, instead, where Leona served for the next 25 years. During her years in Cuba, Leona was sent home on three furloughs due to illness. She is remembered as one who resisted furloughs as she feared the church leaders at home would consider her frail condition reason enough to prohibit her return. While in Cuba, Leona taught and preached the Bible while often teaching English to support herself and to qualify to remain in the country.

Life for Leona was not easy in Cuba. The culture resisted the efforts of a single woman preacher. A visit by Rev. H. F. Reynolds, general superintendent, in March of 1916, soon after the Pentecostal Church of the Nazarene took over the work in Cuba, greatly encouraged her. She wrote to him inviting him to revisit Cuba and recounting seven ways his first visit had built up the work. Leona's second point reads: "It [Reynolds's visit] gave *authority to woman's work* as they are called and sent of God; thus, removing prejudice from the minds of our own people on that line." Later in the letter she continues, "I have had to labor here against so many prejudices against women preaching and against anything of an emotional nature, any manifestation of God's Spirit through my emotional nature that it has been very hard for me."[18]

Joining with the Nazarenes gave Leona increased determination to continue in her work despite opposition. Little is known firsthand of her achievements in Cuba, but when missionaries returned to Cuba years later they met those who had been deeply impacted by her efforts. Several of those converted under her tutelage formed the core of the Nazarene work decades after her departure.

A Methodist missionary remembered Leona by saying, "If all the Nazarenes are like Leona Gardner they are certainly a wonderful people." When the new missionaries, Lyle and Grace Prescott, were traveling by train to Trinidad they met James Jorge, Leona's adopted son, by then an adult and respected employee of United States Steel in Havana. He told the Prescotts, "I owe everything to Leona Gardner and the Church of the Nazarene."[19]

In 1927, after her last furlough from Cuba, she was appointed to Guatemala. Leona landed in the city of Salamá on July 8, 1927, where she lived while the resident missionaries were on furlough. Upon their return she moved 20 miles across mountainous terrain to Puruhla, where she became pastor to the native peoples. She lived in a small cane-thatched adobe building where she slept in the backroom and held services in the front.

Early in 1931 her home burned to the ground. One man who met Leona shortly after this event describes Leona and then what happened:

> I met her coming down the street dressed in a long-coated brown suit and a black knitted woolen cap. She did not impress me as the young woman I had heard about. Her face bore the telltale lines of years of faithful labor, and her shoulders were stooped with the burden of 34 years of missionary service . . . The persecution of the Catholics and the threats they made against the little missionary woman were terrible. One night while she was safely locked in her little bedroom and sleeping soundly an Indian crept stealthily up beside the little grass roofed house and set fire to the

roof. Miss Gardner slept on. Being slightly deaf and having a good conscience she was not easily disturbed. The fire burned brightly, lighting up the side of the hill and the road. Across the valley a fiesta was in progress with dancing, and drinking and carousing but they paid no attention to the burning house. Suddenly a believer who lived near by was awakened by the sound of crackling flames. He saw the light and hastily arising ran to Miss Gardner's room. He shouted but she slept on. He pounded on the door until she finally awakened and came out. With the help of some other believers who came most of her belongings were saved. The chapel was practically destroyed.[207]

How Leona recovered from this disaster is unknown, but the earliest report of this incident from a sister missionary shows great confidence in her ability. Leona "is a brave warrior for God; a little white-haired lady of 62 years, delicate of physique, but like the name she has (Leona means lioness) bold in her stand."[21]

A few years later Leona felt she should concentrate her efforts in Flores, Petén, an island town in the middle of Lake Petén, in the wilderness portion of northern Guatemala. A revival a few years earlier had begun the work. While there she discovered how closely connected this area was to British Honduras, so she traveled to Benque Viejo. But while there, her passport expired and she was not allowed back into Guatemala. The elderly missionary did not despair, however; she simply began work in British Honduras, especially among the Guatemalan community that resided in the neighboring nation. She taught, preached, and lived holiness, first from a house with a dirt floor and then from a home and renovated ballroom rented from a wealthy absentee citizen of Benque Viejo. Much of Leona's work required her to travel from town to town in dugout canoes on lakes where furious tropical storms rose with little warning. This petite woman feared little and kept up her missionary work until she was no longer able.

By 1941 Leona, then in her 70s, had come home to the United States. A letter from the office secretary of the General Board of the Church of the Nazarene asked Leona about her ordination status because the board was making adjustment in missionary pensions. It was assumed by most that she was indeed ordained, and she was referred to as "Rev. Gardner" in several articles. Her response, however, revealed that she was never officially ordained, but in her mind she always was. "I am sorry to say that my long residence in the Foreign Field caused me not to have the opportunity for ordination. I did some pastoral work, however, in spiritual things and in preaching for which I was ordained by His Hand according to John 15:16; but I should have appreciated very much the ordination that the Church of the Nazarene would have given me."[22]

Leona Gardner's life was indeed that of a fully qualified minister although she never became an ordained elder. Concluding this history with her story is apt, for she represents all of the other unrecognized women, unmentioned in these pages, who faithfully served the Church of the Nazarene from its earliest years.

Frances McClurkan, Leila Stratton, and Leona Gardner, perhaps more than some of the other women preachers in the early Church of the Nazarene, provide evidence of the hidden lives of other women who served the church when their efforts were officially unacknowledged. Frances McClurkan always claimed she gave "talks" rather than sermons, but those who heard her remember her as a powerful preacher second to none. Leila Stratton remained an itinerant who was enabled to provide leadership to groups close to home who knew her and recognized her gifts. Leona Gardner chose the path that so many other women felt would be their only place for service. She ventured boldly into mission work, living alone for decades in Latin cultures unfriendly to women's religious leadership. But she never gave up.

All three women exemplify the kind of determination it took to serve the church in their day. While Frances Mc-Clurkan's ministry emerged out of her partnership with her itinerant husband, Leila Stratton and Leona Gardner did what they knew they must to remain faithful to their callings wherever they found themselves. This meant Leila evangelizing in small towns throughout the South as she was asked and Leona serving in Cuba and British Honduras when those weren't the countries she was originally sent to. Location didn't matter. When an opportunity presented itself, each of these women rose to the challenge because that is what it took for them to serve the church when the church itself provided few formal opportunities.

6

What It Takes
for Women Ministers
to Survive and Thrive

What Do the Lives of the First Generation of Ordained Women Reveal?

After reading about the lives of these vital women ministers, one may ask, "What do their lives reveal?" A steadfast belief in God's personal call into the preaching ministry provides the common thread that weaves together the lives of these 12 women. Their efforts were enabled by the indwelling of the Holy Spirit that each claimed through sanctification. Divine conviction formed their ministerial identities. Annie Johnson, the first young woman to serve as song evangelist to Mary Lee Harris Cagle, illustrates in a passionate sermon how this deep, defiant conviction sustained the women in ministry: "And no one can be more true to a God-given call to the ministry of the gospel than a woman. Oppose as much as you like, yet women goes preaching on. It may be, my friend, that by your opposition you will keep some soul from God, but you can never affect us in the least. For God said, 'Preach,' and preach we shall."[1]

A second common theme that appears in the lives of at least half of these early women preachers is the struggle to accept the call to preach. Such a call was often thought inappropriate and out of line with the expectations of family, society, and church. Recall Mary Lee Harris Cagle's words from *Women Preachers:* "I knew to go out in this country as a woman preacher would mean to face bitter opposition, prejudice, slanderous tongues, my name cast out as evil, my motives misconstrued."[2] E. J. Sheeks echoes the same fear: "I knew to accept the call to preach meant sacrifice, self-denial, reproach, opposition and persecutions. A very dark picture was before me."[3] None of these women blithely decided one day to preach. An inner transformation had to take place to motivate such countercultural behavior.

It is unknown if Lucy Knott, Maye McReynolds, Santos Elizondo, Elsie Wallace, or Olive Winchester felt inner conflict over their callings. If their inmost thoughts were accessible to us today, it would be a safe guess that they, too, wrestled with God over being asked to step outside of respected spheres of women's influence. In order to actively enter public ministry each of these women had to undergo a conversion of ideology. The crisis of trusting God's call required a transformation, an expansion of what they deemed appropriate behavior for their lives.

A third similarity found in these women's lives is a dedication to action before official sanction or ordination was conferred upon them. Each of these 12 ministers actively preached prior to any licensing or approval. They acted out of conviction whenever opportunity arose, not waiting for appointment by a superintendent or ordination by an assembly. Susan Fitkin's description of her ordination service illustrates this point. She remembers it as a "memorable service but [it] was only the human sanction to God's work."[4]

A fourth parallel in these women's lives is shown by the kinds of churches or organizations they served. Most served as pastors or leaders of organizations they had founded. They did not passively wait for a congregation to recognize their gifts. Lucy Knott began working at the Mateo Street Mission, a preaching point, and developed the work into a fully organized church. Maye McReynolds quit her job and began to work among the Mexican people in Los Angeles, which resulted in the First Mexican Church of the Nazarene. Santos Elizondo gathered family and friends together and started the church in El Paso before doing the same in Juarez. Elsie Wallace turned a street mission into a local church in Spokane. Susan Fitkin served as the first president of what would become the Nazarene World Mission Society. Martha Curry and Olive Winchester worked at the Pentecostal Collegiate Institute during its earliest years. Mary Lee Harris Cagle helped plant most every church she pastored, as did E. J. Sheeks. Frances McClurkan worked side by side with her husband as the Pentecostal Mission was formed. Leila Stratton moved from faithful participation in a local Pentecostal Mission to overseer. Leona Gardner preached and taught in countries where no other Nazarene had gone before. Each woman helped create the social structure in which she ministered.

And the fifth recurrent theme that stands out in the lives of these women is their commitment to upholding their sisters in ministry. In 1891 Martha Curry highlighted the lives of eight women ministers in an article titled "The Women of the Fifth General Assembly." Her closing words express the respect and camaraderie these women shared:

Time and space compel me to stop. I have not mentioned nearly all of them. There is Mrs. Carrie Ann Sloan, Mrs. Stella Crooks, Mrs. Carrie Flower, Mrs. May Taylor Roberts, and a host of others—women who have prayed and wept, traveled and exhorted, preached and sung, and labored together with God in the building up of this, the greatest and mightiest religious movement of the present day.[5]

The intertwining of the lives of these women all point to the same story. In the West Maye McReynolds superintended and advocated for Santos Elizondo. In the East Martha Curry shared the revival platform and worked to keep the Pentecostal Collegiate Institute alive alongside Olive Winchester. Susan Fitkin helped establish an organization through which tens of thousands of women enabled missionaries worldwide. In the Northwest, Elsie Wallace found working at evangelistic meetings with another woman lessened the loneliness. In western Tennessee Mary Lee Harris Cagle and E. J. Sheeks planted churches together. Leila Owen Stratton worked with another woman in following up on local revivals in Lebanon, Tenn., although the extent of the partnership is unknown. Leona Gardner stands as the exception to the rule. What little we know of her life depicts her as the more solitary minister, and whether this was caused by her geographical isolation is hard to determine.[6]

In summary, these women were convicted by the Holy Spirit to preach, they experienced a conversion—a transformation of values—as to what was appropriate as a woman's role in the church, and they acted upon their heartfelt beliefs whether supported by the church or not. They preached when opportunity knocked and often founded new church structures in which they could fulfill their callings. They also worked together, recognizing there was strength and safety in teamwork.

What Happened to the Role of Ordained Women During the Lifetimes of These Women?

Through the lives of these pioneer women preachers useful lessons can be learned about how change—the kind that breaks the status quo—is wrought. They serve as role models who acted as agents of change in a different era, who can inspire present-day women to muster the courage to do likewise. It isn't enough to focus on the inspirational lessons of these lives, however, because they all began their service to the church in an experimental time of its history. During the span of these women's adult lives, the Church of the Nazarene evolved from an experimental holiness movement that countered the established denominations into an acceptable denomination itself. It moved through a time of organization and significant church growth. The period of 1933 to 1958 contained both the greatest upsurge and the onset of the general decline in the ministry of ordained women. Whether or not there is a cause-and-effect relationship between this decline and the increasing institutionalization of the church is debatable. Nonetheless, a simple reading of the section regarding the elder in the *Manual* during this period shows extensive increase in the emphasis on administrative roles.

In the middle of this period, 1945, the Nazarene Theological Seminary opened. Sociologically during this time women tended to be less mobile and economically able to relocate to pursue graduate education, so it is possible that an emphasis on seminary education rather than on the Course of Study taken at home also lessened the numbers seeking ordination by the 1950s.

In the second volume of the denomination's history, author W. T. Purkiser admits that "the story of the Nazarenes provides a critical testing of the thesis that all religious movements necessarily 'run down' in power, zeal, and commitment to essential distinctives"[7] as they mature. Whatever the reasons, there is little doubt that the church has "run down" in its commitment to one of its early distinctives—the ordained ministry of women.

In 1908, when East, West, and South united in Pilot Point, Tex., 13.8 percent of the ordained elders and 15.1 percent of the licensed ministers were women.[8] During the years the first generation of women served the Church of the Nazarene, these percentages increased rather dramatically year by year until the late 1930s and early 1940s when a general decline began. Obviously something was going on in the church or society to discourage women from seeking ordination.

What Discouraged Later Women from Becoming Ministers?

There is no way to fully answer this question. However, a survey of the articles dealing with the topic of women in ministry in the official periodicals of the denomination during this period offers perspective on the pervading cultural concerns.

In 1922, 1934, 1939, and 1943 lay persons raised the question of how the Church of the Nazarene harmonized the ordained ministry of women with the injunctions in 1 Timothy and 1 Corinthians for women to keep silence in the church.[9] Each time, the official answer declared that the calling of the Spirit is not limited by gender or race and that the historical position of ordaining women is faithful to the gospel.

A 1930 article by J. B. Chapman, general superintendent, articulates the denominational defense of women's ministry:

> The fact is that God calls men and women to preach the

gospel, and when He does so call them, they should gladly obey Him and members of the church and of the ministry should encourage and help them in the fulfillment of their task. This is the teaching of the New Testament, the logic of the new dispensation, the position of the Church of the Nazarene.[10]

Chapman's strong advocacy of the rights of women is consistent with the upswing of the numbers of ordained women seen early in the decade of the 1930s. But by 1948 the picture had changed. The official stance of the church had not moved an inch, but society had. Women preachers faced increasing opposition. An anonymous woman pastor was quoted by the editor of the *Herald of Holiness* to highlight the problems women ministers were experiencing. This woman minister cited "a sense of aloneness" as she was the only active woman minister on her district. Listen to her self-description:

[A]t preachers' meetings, assemblies, etc., when the men gather together in informal groups and discussions, and their wives congregate by themselves, I find I am "neither beast, fowl, nor good red herring." Though oftentimes as an afterthought I am invited into some group (usually of the wives) as though they felt, "Poor dear, what *shall* we do with *'her?'*"[11]

This woman minister continued to state the problem of "very few churches being opened to our ministry" and pointed out that each church that called her had previously been served by a woman thus proving "a woman's ability to 'make the grade.'" Lastly she acknowledged the limitations for advancement since most of the people in the pew had not been "educated to the idea that God can work also through a woman pastor, and also due to a subtle sense of perhaps unconscious antagonism, or at least mere tolerance from the church at large."[12]

Her recommendation for beginning to remedy the isolation, prejudice, and lack of opportunity was to create a list of women preachers so that women ministers with similar problems and experiences could encourage and problem solve together.[13] This unknown woman preacher pinpointed the problems that plagued the church by the middle of the 20th century. An ambivalence toward women in the ordained ministry had taken over. The church officially said yes to women seeking ordination while the middle-class culture that dominated the pews said no.

Somehow, somewhere as the church matured, the calling of the Holy Spirit became domesticated. The Spirit that blew at Pentecost still was calling God's daughters to prophesy, but the church of the mid-20th century encouraged women to put family first and then declared the way to do so was to stay at home. For holiness people, the question today remains to be answered, how fully can the Holy Spirit bless the life of a family if one of its members fails to answer the call of God in her life?

In 1950 the September-October issue of *The Preacher's Magazine* was devoted to articles "Of Interest to Women." The opening editorial titled "The Women's Sphere" reveals the double message women were hearing about the ordained ministry. Unwittingly, the editor evidenced a shift in denominational priorities.

The editor acknowledged the inroads women had made into most secular professions since World War II before stating, "Our church has never forbidden women to enter the ministry. It would be honest for us all to confess that such work has not been encouraged, but we are all convinced that God still calls women to be preachers of the gospel." He cites the example of a few ordained women before launching into laudatory praise for pastor's wives and members of the Women's Foreign Missionary Society.[14] These unofficial church roles had become the acceptable and more common ways for women to serve the church. The article then clarified where women really belong: "Of course, the ideal is for the wife to devote herself entirely to the raising of the family, but we are not crying out against these fine women who have been caught in the vise of economic pressure and are accomplishing a dual task."

The editorial ended with a thanksgiving for the loyalty and sacrificial work of the women in the church, and the readers were enjoined not to criticize any calling a woman might have, for it takes everyone's efforts to accomplish the task of spreading the gospel.

Inherent in this editorial is a desire to affirm women in ministry, but the very language shows the ambivalence that characterized the church then and continues today. Rather than positively saying *the Church of the Nazarene always has ordained women,* as J. B. Chapman did in 1930, the author uses the negative, stating *it hasn't forbidden them.* Rather than advocating for and actively helping women to be accepted in the ministry, he says not to criticize those who feel called and to by all means remember that women are best placed in the home unless economic difficulties require outside work. It is clear that the media stereotypes of what families in middle-class, white America were supposed to be like pervaded the church, causing it to cease to be a church that challenged the culture with a new doctrine that could transform society. The Church of the Nazarene had become a guardian of traditional values—the status quo.

What Does This Mean for Women Called to the Ordained Ministry Today?

As of the end of 1992, women comprised 5.8 percent of the total ministerial force (ordained or licensed) of the Church of the Nazarene in the United States and Canada. Of the 377 women elders, only 37 are listed as pastors, and of the 327 listed as licensed ministers, 28 are pastors. This translates to .5 percent of the total ministerial force are women serving pastorates. The majority of women ministers are listed in the denominational records as being "unassigned," available for "pulpit supply," in associate roles, or retired. This means that the female portion of the ministerial force is not being used to its full potential. Because the Church of the Nazarene does not assign ministers to churches, as in an episcopal form of government, the designation "unassigned" is misleading. Perhaps a more apt description would be "few district superintendents are willing to recommend her and few churches are willing to call her as pastor."

The 1992 statistics sadly reveal that the concerns raised by the anonymous woman minister in the article published in 1948 are still of vital concern to the church today. For women serving pastoral roles, isolation continues to be a problem. Many pastoral retreats are still called "Pastors and Wives Retreats," and the woman pastor still finds herself not fully accepted by either category. As there is no denominational forum to gather together ordained women in the ministry, scant opportunities arise for women to discuss how to survive and thrive in the ministry. The lack of churches willing to call a woman pastor still exists because fewer and fewer churches have members who remember when a woman may have led their church in earlier days. This makes the need for educating the laity more crucial than ever.

In 1980 the church added a statement to the appendix of the *Manual* recognizing the rights of women to enter all areas of ministry. Mary Lee Cagle, who fought for such a statement 70 years earlier, would have been pleased even though the statement did not specify the ordained ministry. However, the fact that the statement became necessary points to her early wisdom. Phineas Bresee's argument of "apostolicity" has not been strong enough to guarantee the successful ministry of women in the Church of the Nazarene.

The 1980 statement on "Women's Rights" reads as follows:

> That while man and woman are created equally spiritually in God's sight [Galatians 3:28], that in the interests of the Christian family, moral and ethical standards, Christian modesty and simplicity, we emphasize the distinction as male and female and stress that we respect the God-given distinction so that each may fulfill his or her highest place in the home and in the kingdom of God. We support the right of women to use their God-given spiritual gifts within the church. We affirm the historic right of women to be elected and appointed to places of leadership within the Church of the Nazarene. We oppose any legislation which would be against the scriptural teachings of the place of womanhood in society.[15]

While this statement affirms women's ministry, it fails to advocate it. This statement reads like a nondiscrimination clause that declares the Church of the Nazarene as an equal opportunity employer. It is a statement of "negative affirmation" that says, in part, "Yes, we ordain women, but no, we don't support them in countering social expectations." This ambiguous position supports a woman's ability to hear God's call but does not aid her in fully obeying the divine admonition. It affirms women in helping roles, but it fails them when they are called to prophetic, leadership roles.

It also must be asked of this statement, what are the "scriptural teachings of the place of womanhood in society"? The attention usually given by the church to scriptures that highlight the maternal or domestic roles of women must be held in tension with the absolute demands for equality declared in Gal. 3:28 and Acts 2:17. So it is unfaithful to both scripture and Nazarene history to preach from the pulpit that all are one in Christ and that the Spirit can be poured out upon all flesh and then fail to provide a supportive stance toward the full ministry of women. Pious words without complementary action are empty words.

The biblical witnesses of Miriam, Deborah, Hulda, Abigail, Ruth, Mary of Bethany, Lydia, Priscilla, Phoebe, and the many unnamed women who followed Jesus show that stepping outside of social customs to faithfully serve the people of God is nothing new.

Fortunately, the inclusion of a statement on women's rights in the *Manual* demonstrates that the role of women in the church has become a forefront issue once more. The upswing in the numbers of woman seminarians in the last decade has also helped to resurface the need to advocate for women in the ordained ministry.

General Superintendent William M. Greathouse championed the plight of women in a 1982 editorial:

> The partial eclipse of women ministers in the church of today is lamentable. It reflects the influx of teachings and theologies which are in basic disagreement with our historic biblical position.
>
> The gospel is the Magna Carta for women's ministry. Once again the Lord is pouring out His Spirit on His handmaidens in the Church of the Nazarene and calling them to preach. At least 40 young women are now preparing themselves for various ministries at Nazarene Theological Seminary.[16]

By this statement Dr. Greathouse brings the issue of women in the ordained ministry back full circle to the outpouring of the Holy Spirit, which is where the early women ministers found their power to preach.

Women are still feeling the conviction of a divine calling, just as they did a century ago. Many still face an inner battle to accept the call as socially appropriate before seeking the proper training and preaching for the first time. Perhaps retelling the stories of these early women preachers will enable present-day women preachers to break the cycle of social expectation by encouraging them to speak out and act whether or not they are supported or sanctioned. In cities and towns where the local church is not ready to accept a woman pastor, women clergy may have to pioneer new churches, remind congregations of the historical stance of the Nazarenes toward women, and refute those who fail to interpret scripture fully and fairly in regard to women.

Women, too, must see how important it is to work together. The strength to create a more impartial atmosphere will be found in banding together.

A Personal Witness

Is reading about past role models who advocated a woman's right to full participation in the ministry enough? As a woman, seminary-trained, and reared in the Church of the Nazarene I have found it is not enough. All of the women I have profiled from the first generation of women ministers, with the exception of Frances McClurkan, were deceased before I was born. In my lifetime, I have never had the privilege of having a woman pastor or seeing a female district superintendent preside at a district assembly. One of my most vivid childhood church memories is hearing Nettie Miller, a fiery woman evangelist who held a week-long revival in our church. Unfortunately, she only influenced me during one week of my life.

There were no women on the religion faculty of the Nazarene liberal arts college I attended. When I looked into seminary, I found no women on the faculty of Nazarene Theological Seminary. The proud legacy remained of Wesleyan theologian, Dr. Mildred Bangs Wynkoop,[17] another brilliant woman who influenced the church as did Olive Winchester, but her presence no longer filled the class-room.

The extraordinary intellectual abilities of Mildred Wynkoop and Olive Winchester are uncontested. Yet Naz-arene institutions of higher education cannot wait for the time when new exceptional minds break through the barri-ers to provide role models. One administrator of Nazarene higher education told me when I expressed dismay over the scarcity of women in theological education and the ministry, "Those with extraordinary gifts and calls can make it. The church has historical precedents for women in leadership." The logic of his position baffled me. I retorted, "So, men professing a call who have mediocre abilities have a right to be called by churches or accepted as theo-logical educators, but a woman has to be extraordinary?" He thought for a moment and said, "You have a point."

Indeed, there is a point to be made. God doesn't dis-criminate by gender or race in calling the faithful to public ministry. Why should the church? God doesn't call only those with extraordinary talents. God demands obedience to one's divine calling and a commitment to fully develop and use one's God-given gifts. Why should the church ac-cept only the women with extraordinary abilities?

The foremothers of the Church of the Nazarene taught the church, by word and example, to do better. The time has come for the church to reclaim its proud heritage and to write a new chapter in history—one that affirms, advo-cates, and celebrates the ordained ministry of women.

Notes
Bibliography
and
Recommended
Reading

NOTES

Introduction

1. *Manual of the Church of the Nazarene* (Los Angeles: 1898), 16.

2. John T. Benson, Jr., *Holiness Organized or Unorganized: A History 1898-1915 Pentecostal Mission, Incorporated, Nashville, Tennessee* (Nashville: Trevecca Press, 1977), 223-34. (In the 17-year history [1898-1915] of the Pentecostal Mission, 39% [104 out of 268] of the evangelists licensed were female.)

3. Ibid., 79.

4. The separate sphere ideology will be more fully explained in chapter 1.

5. The first flier used to advertise the first service in what would become Los Angeles First Church of the Nazarene, quoted in Timothy Smith, *Called unto Holiness: The Story of the Nazarenes: The Formative Years* (Kansas City: Nazarene Publishing House, 1962), 111.

Chapter 1

1. By midcentury one-third to one-half of the population of American cities had been born abroad. Mary Ryan, *Womanhood in America: From Colonial Times to the Present* (New York: New Viewpoints, 1979), 108.

2. Margaret Hope Bacon, *Mothers of Feminism: The Story of Quaker Women in America* (San Francisco: Harper and Row, 1986), 105.

3. John Wesley to Sarah Crosby, Mar. 18, 1769, in *The Works of John Wesley*, 3rd ed., 14 vols. (London: Wesleyan Methodist Book Room, 1872; reprint, Kansas City: Beacon Hill Press of Kansas City, 1978), 12:355.

4. Charles White, *The Beauty of Holiness: Phoebe Palmer as Theologian, Revivalist, Feminist, and Humanitarian* (Grand Rapids: Zondervan, 1986), 189.

5. It wasn't until 1869 that Maggie Van Cott became the first woman granted a preacher's license by the Methodist Episcopal church. Full ordination without qualification wouldn't come to the United Methodist church until 1956.

6. White, *Beauty of Holiness*, 190.

7. Ibid.

8. Elizabeth Cazden, *Antoinette Brown Blackwell: A Biography* (Old Westbury, N.Y.: Feminist Press, 1983), 25.

9. Ibid., 26.

10. "Women's Right to Preach the Gospel," reprinted in Donald W. Dayton, ed., *Holiness Tracts Defending the Ministry of Women* (New York: Garland, 1985), 21-22.

11. Phoebe Palmer, *The Way of Holiness with Notes on the Way* (New York: Self-published, 1854), 119.

12. Ibid., 33.

13. Ibid.

14. Palmer quoted in Nancy Hardesty's, *Women Called to Witness* (Nashville: Abingdon, 1984), 95.

15. Phoebe Palmer, *Promise of the Father* (New York: Self-published, 1872), 8.

16. Ibid., 14.

17. Ibid., 1-2.

Chapter 2

1. Smith, *Called unto Holiness,* 94.

2. E[arnest] A[lexander] Girvin, *Phineas F. Bresee: A Prince in Israel* (New York: Garland, 1984), 82, 83. (Originally published by the Pentecostal Nazarene Publishing House, 1916.)

3. Smith, *Called unto Holiness,* 50.

4. Smith, *Called unto Holiness,* 110, quoting the *Los Angeles Times,* October 21, 1895. It should be noted that J. P. Widney withdrew from the Nazarenes in 1899 and returned to Methodism. The emotional fervor that came to characterize many of the Nazarene services was alien to Widney's quiet personal style.

5. Girvin, *Prince in Israel,* 90.

6. Ibid., 114.

7. "Lucy P. Knott," *Herald of Holiness,* (406) p. 14. It should be noted that William S. Knott's obituary cites Lucy's date of sanctification as 1894, one year later than her obituary states.

8. Girvin, *Prince in Israel,* 115.

9. Lucy P. Knott to H. F. Reynolds, September 27, 1913.

10. Lucy P. Knott, "Company E," *Nazarene Messenger* 12, no. 1 (July 4, 1907): 20.

11. Charles Allen McConnel, "Our Slogan and the Envelope System," *The Other Sheep* 2, no. 6 (December 1914): 1.

12. "A Christmas Surprise," *The Joyful Sound,* January 1911.

13. Smith, *Called unto Holiness,* 118.

14. Southern California District Minutes, 1923, 18-19.

15. In an article titled "The Passing of Mrs. A. F. McReynolds," *Herald of Holiness,* March 30, 1932, E. A. Girvin recalls meeting Maye McReynolds during a prayer meeting in October 1899. He claims her sanctification happened "a short time previously" and that she had become an active member of Los Angeles First Church.

16. Mrs. M. McReynolds, in "Quarterly Report of the Nazarene Spanish Mission," December 31, 1910.

17. Mrs. M. McReynolds, "Spanish Mission," *Nazarene Messenger,* June 18, 1908, 4.

18. *Minutes of the Third General Assembly, Pentecostal Church of the Nazarene.* Afternoon Session, Nashville, October 7, 1911.

19. Mrs. M. McReynolds to H. F. Reynolds, June 2, 1925. Nazarene Archives, Kansas City.

20. Ibid.

21. *Journal of the Seventh General Assembly* (1928), 92.

22. Maye McReynolds to the General Missions Board, TL, September 22, 1912. Nazarene Archives.

23. Mrs. Maye McReynolds to the General Missionary Board of the Pentecostal Church of the Nazarene, Chicago, TLS, October 1910. Nazarene Archives.

24. S. D. Athans to H. F. Reynolds, October 5, 1915. Athans Collection, Nazarene Archives.

25. E. Y. Davis to E. G. Anderson, May 15, 1922. Nazarene Archives.

26. E. Y. Davis to H. F. Reynolds, January 31, 1928. Nazarene Archives.

27. *Journal of the Seventh General Assembly* (1928), 92.

28. Rev. J. D. Scott, superintendent, "Mexican Assembly," *Quadrennial Report of the General Board of Foreign Missions* (to the Sixth General Assembly of the Church of the Nazarene), Kansas City, September 1923, 27.

29. Clipping dated December 30 with no year or source cited. Foreign Missions correspondence file for 1926-28. Nazarene Archives.

30. Letter to E. G. Anderson, treasurer, from Santos Elizondo, January 10, 1925.

31. Letter from Santos Elizondo to Mr. J. G. Morrison, executive secretary, Department of Foreign Missions, dated August 12, 1931. Reprinted in *Herald of Holiness*, June 15, 1982, 9.

32. "Border Mexican Work," report of superintendent to the Foreign Missions Department of the General Board, January 5, 1935.

33. Mrs. Guadalupe Elizondo Navarro, "Last Hours of Sister Santos," TD, not dated but received in Kansas City, March 11, 1941. Nazarene Archives.

34. "Rev. Santos Elizondo Passes," *The Other Sheep*, May 1941, 5.

35. Smith, *Called unto Holiness*, 143.

36. Ibid., 7.

37. Mrs. DeLance Wallace, "Spokane, Wash.," *Nazarene Messenger*, January 12, 1902, 10.

38. Unsigned, "Spokane, Wash.," *Nazarene Messenger*, July 24, 1902, 6.

39. *The First Annual Assembly Journal of the Northwest District Church of the Nazarene.* July 4-5, 1905, Spokane, Wash., 5.

40. "History of First Church of the Nazarene, Spokane, Washington, 1902-1977," Seventy-fifth Anniversary pamphlet produced by the church.

41. J. B. McBride, "Walla Walla, Wash.," *The Pentecostal Messenger*, early 1913.

42. DeLance and Elsie M. Wallace to Rev. H. F. Reynolds and wife, March 21, 1911.

43. Alpin Bowes, ed., *Proceedings of the 15th Annual Assembly of the Northwest District of the Pentecostal Church of the Nazarene*, 21, 34.

44. "General Superintendent" to President, C.W.R.&N. Co., TL, March 6, 1920. Nazarene Archives.

45. *Proceedings of the 16th Annual Assembly of the Northwest District of the Pentecostal Church of the Nazarene* (1920), 30.

46. Mrs. D. L. Wallace to Sr. Hawkins, January 24, 1926.

47. "Rev. Mrs. Elsie May Wallace," *Herald of Holiness* [late 1946], 30.

48. Mrs. DeLance Wallace, pastor, "Report to the Annual Meeting of the Church of the Nazarene, Seattle, Wash.," April 4, 1928.

Chapter 3

1. Smith, *Called unto Holiness*, 79.

2. Susan N. Fitkin, *Grace More Abounding: A Story of the Triumphs of Redeeming Grace During Two Score Years in the Master's Service* (Kansas City: Nazarene Publishing House, n.d.), 11.

3. Ibid., 13. (Susan is alluding to Ezek. 3:5-6.)

4. Ibid., 29.

5. Ibid., 36.

6. Ibid., 39.

7. Susie Norris and A. E. Fitkin, "Rosendale, N.Y., March 17," *Christian Witness and Advocate of Bible Holiness*, March 26, 1896, 9.

8. Fitkin, *Grace More Abounding*, 43.

9. Ibid., 46.

10. Ibid., 51.

11. Ibid., 52.

12. Ibid., 64-66.

13. Ibid., 71.

14. "Rev. S. N. Fitkin," Memoirs Committee report presented at the 1956 General Assembly. Susan Fitkin Collection, Nazarene Archives.

15. All material quoted in Martha's words is taken from an undated, typed partial manuscript found by Janet Williams.

16. Seth C. Rees was a Friends minister who founded the International Apostolic Holiness Church that later merged with the Church of the Nazarene. Rees left the denomination over doctrinal differences and a desire for increased congregational autonomy in 1917. The University Church of the Nazarene in Pasadena, Calif., left with Rees and provided the nucleus for the Pentecostal-Pilgrim Church.

17. A. R. Riggs, "Lowell," *Beulah Christian*, March 1902 (Providence, R.I., ed.), 8.

18. Report by D. Rand Pierce in ibid.

19. Alma West to Janet Williams, June 2, 1984. (Alma wrote on behalf of her aged mother.)

20. This response was taken from a survey sent out by Janet Smith Williams. Readers should keep in mind that while authoritative men are often considered good leaders it is not uncommon for authoritative women to be considered "bossy."

21. Mrs. Albert G. Lunn to Ms. Janet Williams, January 27, 1986.

22. "Rev. Martha E. Curry," obituary in *Herald of Holiness*, (916) [March 1949], 20.

23. Association of Pentecostal Churches in America. *Minutes of the 10th Annual Meeting*, held in Malden, Mass., with the Pentecostal Mission Church, Judson Square. April 11-16, 1904, 41.

24. An account of the origins of the church in East Palestine, Ohio, is found in Martha E. Curry, pastor, "East Palestine, Ohio," *Nazarene Messenger*, February 25, 1909, 5.

25. The school at Hutchinson, Kans. began under the auspices of the Apostolic Holiness Church. Mrs. Mattie Hoke and her holiness meeting organized a mission, the Bible school, and held an annual camp meeting. The group joined the Nazarenes in 1909, and the school was later absorbed into the work of Bethany Nazarene College [now Southern Nazarene University] in Bethany, Okla.

26. Letter from Martha E. Curry to Brother Smith dated March 11, 1947. Return address from Lowell, Mass. Found in biographical file on Martha Curry, Nazarene Archives.

27. Association of Pentecostal Churches of America. *Minutes of the Sixth Annual Meeting*, held in the First Pentecostal Church, Chestnut St., Lynn, Mass., April 9-14, 1901 (Providence, R.I.: Pentecostal Printing Co.), 10.

28. The Pentecostal Collegiate Institute began in Saratoga Springs, N.Y., under the leadership of Rev. Lyman C. Pettit, pastor of a Congregational Methodist church. The school later moved to North Scituate, R.I., after charges of fanaticism and unseemly moral conduct doomed the already financially strapped institution. Nonetheless, PCI offered some of the finest instructors ever produced by Nazarene higher education. The school would move once more to Wollaston, Mass., and become Eastern Nazarene College.

29. E. Wayne Stahl, "I Meet a Super-Victor," *Herald of Holiness*, May 26, 1947, 7.

30. *Beulah Christian*, March 1902.

31. The S.T.M. degree is a master of sacred theology and the Th.D. is a doctorate of theology.

32. Olive inherited $25,000 from her great-uncle Oliver Winchester, owner of the Winchester Repeating Arms Company of New Haven, Conn.

33. Undated, unsigned clipping attached to handwritten notes from the Executive Meeting of the Pentecostal Church, dated May 5, 1913.

34. In letters from Ross E. Price (one of Dr. Winchester's students and compiler of a brief biography) to Dr. F. C. Sutherland (president of Northwest Nazarene College in the early 1960s), Price surmises that Winchester moved West after the drowning of the dean of PCI, Ernest Perry. Price claims Winchester and this man were engaged before she returned from Scotland and were soon to be married. Others queried from those early days do not recall that these two were romantically tied. Price claims in a letter dated September 11, 1962, "I know I am right that she was engaged to the young man. And I know that when he drowned she then decided never to marry but to give herself to teaching. Whether she found the situation at North Scituate unattractive for other reasons I cannot say. But I do know it was characteristic of her to make such a move to leave the unhappy past."

35. Document in the biographical file for Olive M. Winchester held in the archives of Northwest Nazarene College library, Nampa, Idaho.

36. Founders' Day Pamphlet, Northwest Nazarene College, September 30, 1966.

37. Dr. Ross E. Price, "Some Data about Miss Olive M. Winchester, Th.D." (Colorado Springs: 1986). Unpublished manuscript, Winchester Collection, College Archives, Point Loma Nazarene College, San Diego.

38. Harvey B. Snyder, Pasadena, Calif., to Ross Price, Kankakee, Ill., ALS, February 19, 1947, reproduced in Price's unpublished manuscript.

39. Bertha Munro to F. C. Sutherland, July 24, 1962.

Chapter 4

1. This new southern holiness sect came into being in 1904 when Jernigan's group, the Independent Holiness Church based in Pilot Point, Tex., joined with the New Testament Church of Christ that began in Milan, Tenn., under Robert Lee Harris.

2. C. B. Jernigan, *Holiness Evangel*, November 1, 1901, 6, quoted in Smith, *Called unto Holiness*, 215.

3. Robert Stanley Ingersol, "Burden of Dissent: Mary Lee Cagle and the Southern Holiness Movement" (Ph.D. diss., Duke University, 1989), 276. (Much of the substance of this chapter comes from his thesis, which is the first full history of women's contributions to one of the merging bodies that formed the Church of the Nazarene.)

4. Smith, *Called unto Holiness*, 220.

5. J. B. Chapman, "October Gleanings," *Herald of Holiness*, October 15, 1930, 5.

6. Ingersol, "Burden of Dissent," 277.

7. Smith, *Called unto Holiness*, 222.

8. Mrs. Fannie McDowell Hunter, ed., "Mrs. Mary Lee Cagle, 'My Call to the Ministry'" in *Women Preachers* (Dallas: Berachah Printing Co., 1904), 70. Reprinted in Dayton, ed., *Holiness Tracts*.

9. Ibid., 71.

10. B. T. Roberts, *Ordaining Women* (Rochester, N.Y.: Earnest Christian Publishing House, 1891), 158-59. Reprinted in Dayton, ed., *Holiness Tracts*.

11. Hunter, ed., *Women Preachers*, 72.

12. Ingersol, "Burden of Dissent," 168.

13. *Government and Doctrines of New Testament Church* (Milan, Tenn.: Printed at the Exchange Office, 1903), 10.

14. Ingersol, "Burden of Dissent," 221.

15. Hamlin District of the Church of the Nazarene, *Proceedings*, report of the District Evangelist (pp. 28-29) quoted in Ingersol, "Burden of Dissent," 291.

16. Mary Lee Cagle to E. J. Fleming, December 16, 1938, quoted in Ingersol, "Burden of Dissent," 284.

17. Mrs. E. J. Sheeks, "Christian Experience and Call to Preach," in Hunter, ed., *Women Preachers*, 85.

18. Ibid.

19. Ibid.

20. Elliott J. Sheeks to Mrs. R. B. Mitchum, March 22, 1935. E. J. Sheeks Collection in the Nazarene Archives.

21. Quotes from Mrs. E. J. Sheeks, "Christian Experience and Call to Preach," in Hunter, ed., *Women Preachers*.

22. E. J. Sheeks to Hazel Mitchum, September 6, 1901, and E. J. Sheeks to Mrs. R. B. Mitchum, September 7, 1901.

23. *Pentecostal Herald,* June 8, 1904, 14.

24. Mrs. E. J. Sheeks, "From Banner, Miss.," *Pentecostal Herald,* July 20, 1904, 7.

25. J. D. Thurmond, "From Pine Valley, Miss.," *Pentecostal Herald,* August 17, 1904.

26. E. J. Sheeks letter to Bro. Upchurch dated March 20, 1905, and reprinted in *The Purity Journal,* April 1905.

27. E. J. Sheeks to Mrs. R. B. Mitchum, March 22, 1935. Donie Mitchum Collection, Nazarene Archives.

Chapter 5

1. In 1898 there was not a denominational consciousness on the part of the founders. The organization began as the Pentecostal Alliance and was aligned with the Christian and Missionary Alliance. When the Nashville group went independent in 1901 it changed the name to Pentecostal Mission. By 1915 it was a denomination that licensed and ordained ministers throughout the Southeast.

2. Premillennialism carries a view of Christ's imminent return that often discourages the organization of formal institutions or concentration on the longevity of an organization, for Jesus is expected any day.

3. "A Beautiful Tribute to Mrs. J. O. McClurkan from Her Daughter, Mrs. Merle Heath," *The Messenger* (periodical of Trevecca Nazarene College, Nashville), December 1941, 1.

4. Merle McClurkan Heath, *A Man Sent of God: The Life of J. O. McClurkan* (Kansas City: Beacon Hill Press, 1947), 24.

5. Ibid., 31.

6. Ibid., 23.

7. Ibid., 81.

8. Ibid., 82.

9. "Widow of Founder First Church Nashville," *Nazarene Weekly* 37 (June 26, 1966): 1.

10. Leila Owen Stratton, "Good Tidings of Great Joy," *Living Water,* October 22, 1903.

11. D. C. Vaughter, *Living Water,* September 17, 1908, 12.

12. Leila Owen Stratton, "Wilford, Stratton's Corner," *Living Water,* November 18, 1909, 12-13.

13. Report from Mrs. Lee Tatum, *Living Water,* September 1, 1904.

14. Leila Owen Stratton, *Living Water,* October 27, 1910, 12.

15. Benson, *Holiness Organized or Unorganized,* 175.

16. Hester Ann Rogers was one of the early Methodist women in England who traveled throughout England leading prayer meetings, classes, and prayer bands. Her spiritual autobiography and collected letters were reprinted in the United States in the 19th century. It is to one of these works that Leona is probably referring.

17. Leona Gardner, Undated biographical sketch, ADS. Leona Gardner Collection, Nazarene Archives. (All further firsthand recollections in this chapter are from the same source unless otherwise noted.)

18. Leona Gardner, Trinidad, Cuba, to Rev. H. F. Reynolds, Cobán, Guatemala, ALS, March 22, 1916. 1916 Foreign Mission Collection, Nazarene Archives.

19. Stephen S. White, "Editorial: Working with Leona Gardner," *Herald of Holiness,* October 28, 1953, 12-13.

20. Rev. R. W. Birchard, "A Missionary Heroine of Guatemala," *The Other Sheep,* December 1935, 20-21.

21. Pearle Ingram, "Sister Gardner Escaped from Burning House," *The Other Sheep,* March 1931, 9.

22. Leona Gardner, Campo, Calif., to Miss Emma B. Word, Kansas City, ALS, April 11, 1941. World Missions Collection, Nazarene Archives.

Chapter 6

1. Mrs. Annie May Fisher, "A Woman's Right to Preach: A Sermon Reported and Delivered at Chilton, Texas" (San Antonio: Self-published, n.d.).

2. Hunter, ed., *Women Preachers,* 71.

3. Ibid., 85.

4. Fitkin, *Grace More Abounding,* 46.

5. Martha E. Curry, "The Women of the Fifth General Assembly," *Herald of Holiness,* October 8, 1919, 9.

6. It should also be noted that several of these women—Elsie Wallace, Susan Fitkin, Mary Lee Harris Cagle, and Frances McClurkan—served in ministerial capacities with their ordained husbands. Lucy Knott served as an associate pastor with her son, J. Proctor Knott, for many years. Perhaps having family support lessened the need for collaboration that the others readily sought through working side by side with other women ministers.

7. W. T. Purkiser, *Called unto Holiness,* vol. 2, *The Second Twenty-five Years, 1933-58* (Kansas City: Nazarene Publishing House, 1983), 311.

8. Statistics compiled from the 1908 General Assembly Minister Records. There were 59 women elders out of a 427 total elders (13.8%) and 26 women licensed ministers out of 172 total licensed ministers (15.1%).

9. "Questions Answered," *Herald of Holiness,* May 3, 1922, 3; J. B. Chapman, "October Gleanings," *Herald of Holiness,* October 15, 1930, 5; "The Question Box," *Herald of Holiness,* February 28, 1934, 5; J. B. Chapman, "The Question

Box," *Herald of Holiness*, February 25, 1939, 14; J. B. Chapman, "The Question Box," *Herald of Holiness*, November 1, 1943, 2.

10. J[ames] B[laine] Chapman, "October Gleanings," *Herald of Holiness*, October 15, 1930, 5.

11. "A Woman Pastor Writes," *Herald of Holiness*, June 21, 1948, 12.

12. Ibid.

13. Ibid.

14. In 1952, the Women's Foreign Missionary Society changed its name to the Nazarene World Missionary Society in hope of gathering men to its ranks. The name change did not succeed in doing so.

15. *Manual of the Church of the Nazarene* (Kansas City: Nazarene Publishing House, 1985), 283.

16. William M. Greathouse, "Women in Ministry: An Editorial," *Herald of Holiness*, June 15, 1982, 1.

17. Mildred Bangs Wynkoop taught theology at Trevecca Nazarene College and Nazarene Theological Seminary over several decades and authored *Theology of Love*, a standard text on Wesleyan holiness theology. Dr. Wynkoop is retired and in failing health.

BIBLIOGRAPHY

Association of Pentecostal Churches in America. *Minutes . . .* of the Annual Meetings. 1901, 1904.

Bacon, Margaret Hope. *Mothers of Feminism: The Story of Quaker Women in America.* San Francisco: Harper and Row Publishers, 1986.

Benson, John T., Jr. *Holiness Organized or Unorganized: A History 1898-1915 Pentecostal Mission, Incorporated, Nashville, Tennessee.* Nashville: Trevecca Press, 1977.

Beulah Christian. March 1902.

Cazden, Elizabeth. *Antoinette Brown Blackwell: A Biography.* Old Westbury, N.Y.: Feminist Press, 1983.

Chafe, William H. *The American Woman: Her Changing Social, Economic and Political Roles, 1920-1970.* New York: Oxford Press, 1972.

Church of the Nazarene Archives. Biographical Files on: Mary Lee Harris Cagle, Martha F. Curry, Santos Elizondo, Susan N. Fitkin, Leona Gardner, Lucy P. Knott, Maye McReynolds, Donie Mitchum, E. J. Sheeks, Leila Owen Stratton, Elsie Wallace. World Mission Files: Juarez, Mexico 1916-28.

Church of the Nazarene. *Proceedings of the . . . General Assembly.* 1911, 1923, 1956.

Church of the Nazarene. Southern California District. *Proceedings of the District Assemblies,* 1898-1950.

Church of the Nazarene. Abilene/Hamlin District. *Proceedings of the District Assemblies,* 1909-1950.

Church of the Nazarene. Northwest District. *Proceedings of the District Assemblies,* 1919-1920.

Dayton, Donald W., ed. *Holiness Tracts Defending the Ministry of Women.* New York: Garland, 1985.

————. "Millennial Views and Social Reform in Nineteenth Century America." *The Coming Kingdom: Essays in American Millennialism and Eschatology.* M. Darrol Bryand and Donald W. Dayton, eds. Barrytown, N.Y.: New Era Books, 1983.

Executive Meeting of the Pentecostal Church of Scotland (handwritten minutes), May 5, 1913.

First Annual Assembly Journal of the Northwest District Church of the Nazarene. Spokane, Wash. July 4-5, 1905.

Fitkin, S[usan] N[orris]. *Grace Much More Abounding: A Story of the Triumphs of Redeeming Grace During Two Score Years in the Master's Service.* Kansas City: Nazarene Publishing House, n.d..

————, and A[bram] E. Fitkin. "Rosendale, N.Y., March 17." *Christian Witness and Advocate of Bible Holiness.* March 26, 1898.

Founders Day pamphlet. Northwest Nazarene College. September 30, 1966.

Girvin, E[rnest] A[lexander]. *Phineas F. Bresee: A Prince in Israel: A Biography.* Kansas City: Pentecostal Nazarene Publishing House, 1916; reprint, New York: Garland, 1984.

Hardesty, Nancy. *Women Called to Witness.* Nashville: Abingdon Press, 1984.

Heath, Merle McClurkan. *A Man Sent of God: The Life of J. O. McClurkan.* Kansas City: Beacon Hill Press, 1947.

————. "A Beautiful Tribute to Mrs. J. O. McClurkan from Her Daughter, Mrs. Merle Heath." *The Messenger* (periodical of Trevecca Nazarene College, Nashville), December 1941.

Herald of Holiness, May 3, 1922; October 15, 1930; March 30, 1932; February 28, 1934; February 25, 1939; November 1, 1943; June 21, 1948; October 28, 1953; June 15, 1982.

"History of First Church of the Nazarene, Spokane, Washington, 1902-1977." Seventy-fifth Anniversary pamphlet.

Hunter, Fannie McDowell, ed. *Women Preachers.* Dallas: Berachah Printing Co., 1904. Reprinted in *Holiness Tracts Defending the Ministry of Women.* Donald W. Dayton., ed. New York: Garland, 1985.

Ingersol, Robert Stanley. "Burden of Dissent: Mary Lee Cagle and the Southern Holiness Movement." Ph.D. diss., Duke University, 1989.

Journal of the Seventh General Assembly of the Church of the Nazarene, 1928.

Knott, Lucy P. "A Christmas Surprise." *The Joyful Sound,* January 1911.

Living Water, October 22, 1903; September 17, 1908; November 19, 1909; October 27, 1910.

Manual of the Church of the Nazarene. Los Angeles, 1898.

Nazarene Messenger, January 12, 1902; November 5, 1903; June 18, 1908; February 25, 1909.

New Testament Churches. "Government and Doctrines." Milan, Tenn.: Exchange Office, 1903.

Northwest Nazarene College Archives. Olive M. Winchester files.

The Other Sheep, December 1914, March 1931, December 1935.

Palmer, Phoebe. *Promise of the Father.* New York: Self-published, 1872.

————. *The Way of Holiness with Notes on the Way.* New York: Self-published, 1854.

Pentecostal Herald, June 8, 1904; August 17, 1904.

Point Loma Nazarene College Archives. Olive Winchester Collection, Southern California District Collection, San Diego.

Price, Ross E. "Some Data about Miss Olive M. Winchester, Th.D." Written in Colorado Springs: 1986. Unpublished manuscript, Olive Winchester Collection, College Archives, Point Loma Nazarene College.

The Purity Journal. April 1905.

Purkiser, W. T. *Called unto Holiness: The Second Twenty-five Years.* Vol. 2. Kansas City: Nazarene Publishing House, 1983.

Roberts, B. T. *Ordaining Women*. Rochester, N.Y. Earnest Christian Publishing House, 1891. Reprinted in Donald W. Dayton, ed., *Holiness Tracts Defending the Ministry of Women*. New York: Garland, 1985.

Ryan, Mary. *Womanhood in America: From Colonial Times to the Present*. New York: New Viewpoints, 1979.

Smith, Timothy L. *Called unto Holiness: The Story of the Nazarenes: The Formative Years*. Kansas City: Nazarene Publishing House, 1962.

———. *Revivalism and Social Reform: American Protestantism on the Eve of the Civil War*. Baltimore: Johns Hopkins University Press, 1957, 1980.

Stahl, E. Wayne. "I Meet a Super-Victor." *Herald of Holiness*, May 26, 1947.

Wallace, Mrs. DeLance. "Report to the Annual Meeting of the Church of the Nazarene, Seattle, Wash." April 4, 1928.

White, Charles Edward. *The Beauty of Holiness: Phoebe Palmer as Theologian, Revivalist, Feminist, and Humanitarian*. Grand Rapids: Zondervan Publishing House, 1986.

"Widow of Founder First Church Nashville." *Nazarene Weekly* 37 (June 26, 1966).

RECOMMENDED READING

Scripture and Women

Bristow, John Temple. *What Paul Really Said About Women: An Apostle's Liberating Views on Equality in Marriage, Leadership, and Love*. San Francisco: Harper-Collins, 1988.

Deen, Edith. *All of the Women of the Bible*. San Francisco: Harper and Row, 1955, 1983.

Hardesty, Nancy, and Letha Scanzoni. *All We're Meant to Be*. Nashville: Abingdon, 1972.

Howe, E. Margaret. *Women and Church Leadership*. Grand Rapids: Zondervan, 1982.

Trible, Phyllis. *Texts of Terror: Literary-Feminist Readings of Biblical Narratives*. Philadelphia: Fortress, 1984.

Weems, Renita. *Just a Sister Away: A Womanist Vision of Women's Relationships in the Bible*. San Diego: LuraMedia, 1988.

Church History and Women

Andrews, William L., ed. *Sisters of the Spirit: Three Black Women's Autobiographies of the Nineteenth Century*. Bloomington, Ind.: Indiana University Press, 1986.

Hardesty, Nancy. *Women Called to Witness: Evangelical Feminism in the 19th Century*. Nashville: Abingdon, 1984.

Hassey, Janette. *No Time for Silence: Evangelical Women in Public Ministry Around the Turn of the Century*. Grand Rapids: Zondervan, 1986.

———. *Women and Religion in America. 1900-1968: A Documentary History* (Vol. 3) San Francisco: Harper and Row, 1986.

Ruether, Rosemary Radford, and Rosemary Skinner Keller, eds. *Women and Religion in America. The Nineteenth Century: A Documentary History* (Vol. 1). San Francisco: Harper and Row, 1981.